A Game for Life
Golf's Rules and Rewards

A Game for Life
Golf's Rules and Rewards

Gene Westmoreland

TATRA PRESS LLC

Library of Congress Control Number: 2012937065

Contact Chris Sulavik
Tatra Press LLC
292 Spook Rock Road
Suffern, NY 10901
www.tatrapress.com

Jacket design by Kathleen Lynch, Black Kat Design.
Book design by Isabella Piestrzynska, Umbrella Graphics.
Distributed by Midpoint Trade Press.

Printed in the United States of America.

ISBN: 9780981932149

To Mary, Mychal, Jay, golf associations and the good guys.
May future generations reap all of golf's rewards!

Table of Contents

Preface

I LOVE GOLF. I LOVE THE CHALLENGE OF A BEAUTIFULLY strategic hole and the joy of a perfectly struck shot. I love the "walk in the park" and try not to let a poor shot interfere with my joy of the hawks and dogwoods, the azaleas and the occasional red fox. I get excited playing a perfectly conditioned course and applaud the efforts of golf course superintendents to provide the best playing conditions possible in great harmony with the environment. I love the courtesy that golf brings to the human condition. People who might cut you off on the highway are often transformed into perfect gentlemen on the course. I love being associated with a sport that involves so many volunteers and does so much for its community. The NFL properly boasts of its charitable efforts, but even they pale when compared to what the PGA Tour and the collective charitable outings produce at "every course USA." I love teaching the Rules of Golf and sincerely believe that every golfer who makes an effort to learn the Rules will enjoy the game just a little more and gain respect for golf's culture, history and traditions at the same time. Golf is a great "revealer" of character and regularly turns strangers on the 1st tee into friends by the 18th green—I treasure the friends the game has provided. I love the *Spirit of Golf*: "All players should conduct themselves in a disciplined manner, demonstrating courtesy and sportsmanship at all times, irrespective of how competitive they may be."

Best of all, perhaps, golf is a lifetime game open to everyone. From 3-hole events, for those too small to carry their own bag, to super-seniors enjoying the company of old friends and reliving past stories and glories, the game eliminates no one. Even those regularly relegated to right field for their company softball games, rode the pines during intramural basketball or as young girls viewed the experience as intimidating can enjoy, and compete, perhaps even beat the stud athletes they once admired, because of golf's unique and effective handicap system.

One of my most memorable rounds was played in Acapulco, Mexico with Greg Jones, then Executive Director of the Disabled Golfers of America. Polio had taken its toll on Greg as a kid but golf became a passion for him, and for thousands of disabled Americans, as adults. Just as important the "First Tee" now brings equipment, instruction and life-changing opportunity to inner-city youngsters. The game can take you around the world and bring you into contact with people from every walk of life.

Whether it is business golf, serious competition or a game with your family or your "regulars" you can feel confident that the application of golf's etiquette and a basic understanding of its rules will consistently make for a fun experience.

I got my start in golf as a caddie at the age of 14. My neighbor and good friend John Callahan bragged that he had pocketed $5.00 in one day working as a single caddie at Harrison Country Club in Harrison, New York, while I was lucky to net $10 for the entire week delivering the Daily Item to about 100 subscribers six days a week. Truth be told, it was as much the chance to take up another sport as it was the money because John told me that caddies were allowed to play the course every Monday on "Caddie Day." In those early years discovering the game, I also made strong friendships and met people who probably helped shape my character. Looking back after all these years, I see how fortunate I was, for example, to have toiled under the very "old school" Caddie Master, J.J. Giandurco.

I took to the game quickly, winning the Junior Caddie Tournament within a few years and saving enough money to pay what was left of my college tuition after being awarded some partial academic and athletic scholarships. That caddie yard was pretty talented. John became a life-long golf pro and is now regarded as one of the game's top-100 instructors, and the senior caddie finalists—the same year I won the junior—both went on to long and successful careers as head golf professionals in the very competitive Metropolitan New York market.

My first lesson with the Rules of Golf came early in my first year as a caddie when I overheard Mrs. Machover remind Mrs. Menicoff that she could not take a practice swing in the bunker. I wished I had memorized my grammar school times-tables and spelling lessons as well as Mrs. Machover's Rules tip, for it was many years before I realized that Mrs. M was wrong! You can take all the practice swings you want in a bunker—and anywhere else for that matter. What she meant was, you can't ground your club in a bunker (or any hazard). I have long since forgiven Mrs. Machover—it turned out she got her Rules education the same way many women do—from their husbands—and most of the husbands got theirs from golfing buddies and caddies.

Rules books are readily available and Rules Seminars are, too, but everyday Rules are miss-applied every day. When is the last time you heard someone insist that you "always go to the nearest side of the cart path to take relief" or "as long as you declare your original ball lost you can go ahead and play your perfectly placed provisional" or "if you break a branch or clip off a leaf on a practice swing you are penalized" or "if you have more than 14 clubs in your bag you can avoid penalty by turning the extra club upside-down in your bag."

Some of these "tips" might be true—but only coincidently. Why the misinformation? Are the Rules too complex? Complex perhaps, but necessarily so, because we all want there to be a Rule to cover every unusual situation such as when a dog scampers off with your ball in his mouth just as your best drive of the day comes to rest. We want a Rule that will penalize an opponent who insists on improving his lie in the rough while "just making sure it was my ball."

I hope you enjoy this gentle approach to the Rules and reap the many rewards the game regularly provides.

—*Gene Westmoreland, Bronxville, New York, 2012*

° PART ONE

Embracing the Spirit of the Rules—Both Written and Unwritten

The Good Golfer

WHAT'S A "GOOD" GOLFER? HOW WOULD YOU DEFINE it? Is it someone who simply shoots low scores, or somebody who plays the game the right way? For me, it's someone who practices good etiquette, someone who's fun to be around, for whom pace of play is not a challenge and someone who's a pleasure to be with on the golf course; that's my definition of a good golfer.

You can be a fun golf partner for anyone. Even very good players are happy to play with an average player if that person is ready to play; knows where to stand; plays by the Rules; doesn't need repeated help finding his ball and, most important, doesn't cry about playing poorly.

My definition of a good golfer is a person who enjoys the game for all the wonderful things it gives us in return.

Companionship, competition and exercise come quickly to mind. But the game also gives us a perfect excuse for a walk in the park and the perfect opportunity to enjoy a beautiful spring morning or a peaceful autumn afternoon. And, we never tire of, or conquer, the challenges presented by the architect, the course superintendent and Mother Nature.

As we wade into a new century we should all be mindful of golf's wonderful traditions and the joy we extract from the game and its environment so that we can pass the game along—intact—to those who will carry it to new heights in the twenty-first century. So, while other sports applaud, if not honor, obnoxious behavior by its stars—behavior mimicked and even "refined" by its rookies—as golf *veterans*, we must accept the position of role models as we introduce the game to our children and grandchildren and welcome newcomers to the game.

In that spirit, the next time you tee it up with a new member or get paired with a beginner, make it a playing lesson. Help them to understand that golf is an examination of the whole person, every facet of human development—physical, intellectual, behavioral and emotional. Golf is not just a long-drive contest where the prize goes to the one with the biggest biceps or even the best hand-eye coordination. It's much more than that. It's a test of our intellect, but it goes way beyond electing strategy or calculating the effects of the wind, the firmness of the turf, the texture of the sand and the slope of the greens. It demonstrates our ability to get along with people—friends and strangers alike—and how to adjust to changing conditions and personalities. Golf is one of the few games where self-reporting of violations is common and success is based on your character and your ability to control your emotions. Pumping adrenalin is seldom an asset and a desire to retaliate against an opponent almost always works against your goals.

In most other major sports, etiquette, if there is any, is a custom. Not so in golf, where etiquette and good fellowship are an elemental part of the game. In fact, Section I of the *Rules of Golf* deals exclusively with etiquette. Think about your favorite golfing companions, those you probably consider "successful golfers." They are almost always the ones who are mindful and respectful of others on the course and, out of consideration for other players, do not hit when someone is within range, or move or talk, stand too close or directly behind the ball or the hole when a player is addressing his ball or making a stroke. Successful golfers also care for the course by smoothing holes and footprints in the bunkers and replacing divots, fixing ball marks and taking care that those who follow will have the same, or better, conditions than they had.

We encourage newcomers, especially the young, to take advantage of the many "teaching moments." We explain, for example, the value of dressing for success, as their next pairing might very well include a future employer! And we should always be aware that, as their role models, if we don't pass along what has made us successful golfers, they will not enjoy all the rewards the game has to offer.

Golf is the perfect game for the twenty-first century—a test of the whole person. Talent will always win tournaments and, while the purely physical test, the ability to belt the ball a mile, will have an important place, it will never define the successful golfer. It takes a whole lot more.

A Remarkable, Fluid Document

There may exist among some a perception that the Rules are impenetrable, inflexible, and that they are meant to be that way—designed, or at least written, to confuse, confound and frustrate golfers. Nothing could be further from the truth. Were this the case, to pick an extreme example, we might still be teeing up our drives a club length from the hole just completed, as was once the norm. Or, to take relief, we might still be required to stand erect, face the hole and drop the ball over the shoulder, as rules prescribed before 1984. The conventions of golf continue to evolve as befits a game of near infinite variety and change. The Rules could hardly be said to be a "closed book" at all.

The *Rules of Golf* is a remarkable, fluid document that is regularly appraised, discussed and debated, and when warranted, altered and amended. I mention this only to highlight the extraordinary relationship and spirit of cooperation that exists between the United States Golf Association (USGA) and the Royal and Ancient (R&A) in Scotland. It was 1952, when the first uniform code of Rules was written by their combined genius. Since then the Rules have been updated every four years—an enviable record of collaboration. To their credit, on behalf of the greater good of the game, the USGA and R&A have never shown reluctance to sit down and talk over their concerns, to, as they say, "take a meeting."

❧

The Rules Book: Your 15th Club...and How to Use It

The Rules of Golf are too complex!
I can never find anything in the Rules book!
Why do the Rules have to be so confusing?

You've heard these laments many times, and have perhaps uttered them yourself, which is curious when you consider that the Rules of Golf actually started out pretty simply: (1) Play the course as you find it; (2) Play your ball as it lays; (3) If you can't do either, do what's fair.

The Rules are more complex today than in the past. And necessarily so. There were no golf carts, cart paths, ball washers, bunker rakes, irrigation boxes and yardage markers in golf's early years. But I, for one, still find the Rules of Golf to be a monument to logic that strives to be consistent and fair.

In other sports, we rely on "experts" to make the calls on what's fair. In golf, we're usually our own referee—and frustration arrives when we can't find the applicable Rules quickly. Why? It's simply a matter of taking the time to learn how to use the Rules book.

The very nature of this great outdoor sport makes the Rules complex, and the desire to keep the book pocket size requires a concisely written document. So, don't waste your time trying to memorize the Rules. Just learn how to use the book.

Here are some steps to help:

Step One: Speak the language of golf. Know the definitions of the basic golf vocabulary. Everyone knows what a sand trap, a lake or a pin is, right? But when a ball is lost in that trap or lake, or when a putt strikes an unattended pin, you'll be hard-pressed to find the applicable Rule unless you use the terms *bunker, water hazard* and *flagstick.*

Some of golf's language may seem outdated (or charming, depending on your point of view), but "talking the talk" is critical. Most players are familiar enough with the terms *match play* and *stroke play* to know that the Rules vary according to the "forms of play." They know that major infractions are handled with a loss of a hole in match play, or a two stroke penalty in stroke play. Notice that the correct term is *stroke play.* The term *medal play* is used regularly, but you wouldn't find a reference to it in the Rules book.

Even match play and stroke play have sub-species. Was it *singles* or *four-ball*? We all know that singles match play means a player against an *opponent*. There are no *opponents* in stroke play: each player competes in a "field" of "competitors."

Four-ball is not as well understood and is often confused with *best ball* or *best ball of four*. In golf-speak, a four-ball match pits a team (or *side*) of two players who play their better ball against the better ball of two other players. *Best-ball* is different. It pits a single player against the better ball of two or the best ball of three opponents. *Best ball of four* is exactly what the name implies.

The term *foursome* may be the most misused in golf. Our game is traditionally played in "groups" of two, three or four. A *group of four* does not, according to the Rules, mean the same thing as foursome. Foursome is a form of play in which a side (team) is made up of two players and the side plays only *one ball* with the partners playing strokes alternately during the play of each hole.

Understanding the different *forms of play* is mandatory if you want to learn and understand the Rules. So are the definitions.

The Rules book is divided into three sections. Section I deals with Etiquette, Section II with Definitions, and Section III with the Rules of Play. Just as before you play golf, you should first appreciate and know the etiquette of the game, before you try to apply the Rules of play, you must appreciate, know and master its definitions.

What's the difference between a _caddie_ and a _forecaddie_; a _water hazard_ and a _lateral water hazard_? When is a ball _holed_, when has it _moved_, and what constitutes a _stroke_? The answers to these and many other potentially misleading terms are found in the 13 pages of definitions near the front of every Rules book.

Take the time to learn and understand the definitions. You'll be amazed how many answers to tricky questions are found right there.

Step Two: Establish all the facts before you go to the book. Where did the incident occur? From a Rules perspective, every course is divided into four distinct areas: _teeing grounds_, _putting greens_ and _hazards_ (bunkers and water hazards) should all sound familiar. The rest of the course is properly referred to as _through the green_. The answer to most Rules questions often depends on _where_ (which part of the course) the incident occurred. Next, consider _who_ was involved. It usually involves the player and sometimes his or her caddie, but at times it may involve the player's partner or *his* caddie, or perhaps his opponent, a fellow competitor or an *outside agency* might have been involved as well?

Step Three: Use the Table of Contents and Index. Don't frustrate yourself by aimlessly flipping through the pages. The Table of Contents shows how the Rules are organized. A look at the captions under each Rule lists the items covered and the order in which they are discussed. You'll often be able to find the relevant Rules simply by referring to the Table of Contents. If you still can't find what you are looking for, your next step should be a trip to the Index.

Consider the Rules book your 15th club. It's a great advantage, but only if you know how to use it. As an example, let's say your ball is accidentally kicked and moved during a search. First, establish all the facts. Where did it happen? Through the green? In a hazard? Who kicked the ball? The player himself? His caddie? What form of play? Match play? Stroke play? Four-ball?

Now, using these key phrases, go to the book's Table of Contents, where we'll find the section "Ball Moved, Deflected or Stopped." The sub-captions offer two choices: Ball at Rest Moved or Ball in Motion, Stopped or Deflected. Your choice should be obvious and you'll be directed to page

75, where you'll find Rule 18 (Ball at Rest Moved). Some of the choices you'll find are:

- Rule 18-1 By an Outside Agency
- Rule 18-2 By Player, Partner, Caddie or Equipment
- Rule 18-3 By Opponent, Caddie or Equipment in Match Play
- Rule 18-4 By Fellow Competitor, Caddie, or Equipment in Stroke Play
- Rules 18-5 By Another Ball

If everyone involved agreed that the ball was moved by *your* caddie *through the green* in *match play*, you'd simply read Rule 18-2 and learn that you incurred a one-stroke penalty and are required to replace your ball. You could have found the same ruling through the Index, by using similar key words and phrases.

Here's another example: After a heavy rainstorm your opponent's ball lies on dry ground but in a divot hole. In order to play his stroke, he has to stand in a wet area. There is no visible water before he takes his stance, but when he addresses the ball, a little water surfaces around the edge of his shoes. He claims he is entitled to relief, but you're not so sure.

Let's establish the facts. The incident occurred *through the green* and involves only the *player* himself. This time, go to the Index. What is the key word or phrase? You might think of choosing *casual water* or *stance*—either one will lead you to the correct ruling. If you went to "casual water," you'll be referred to Rule 25. If you went to "stance" you'll be presented with seven choices. Choice number five reads: "Interference with (your stance by) Casual Water, Ground Under Repair, etc." and refers you to Rule 25-1a.

Casual water is defined as "any temporary accumulation of water (outside of a water hazard) that is *visible* before or after a player takes his stance." Rule 25 says that a player has interference even if the ball is dry and the casual water interferes only with his stance. Your opponent is entitled to relief.

One final situation: Let's say your birdie putt stops on the lip of the hole, but you know it will fall if you wait long enough. You stare and swear and the ball finally falls—but it takes almost a *minute*. What's your score for the hole?

Although you can get to every Rule through either the Table of Contents or the Index, you'll often find that, depending on the question, one is easier than the other. For this question you're better off using the Index where any one of several key phrases—"Ball," "Holed" and "Putting Green"—will all lead you to Rule 16-2 (Ball Overhanging Hole). Once you read the Rules, you'll know the ruling and you'll know that you have made a par! These examples will be discussed later.

So, let's review the procedure for using the Rules book. Study the definitions so you can speak the language of the game. Establish *who* was involved, *where* it happened and the *form of play*. Then, using key words or phrases, go to the Table of Contents or the Index to look up the Rule.

But before you do anything, buy a copy of the *Rules of Golf* and carry it in your bag and learn how to use it. This will enable you to settle almost any common Rules question. But, when something unusual happens, such as if the ball gets stuck in the flag, or if the flagstick hits the ball, you'll need to go the *Decisions on the Rules of Golf*.

Each year the USGA and the R&A receive thousands of phone calls, emails and letters requesting clarification on the Rules of Golf. To help players understand how Rules should be applied and interpreted, the USGA and R&A developed another comprehensive book called *Decisions on the Rules of*

Golf. Etiquette, definitions and Rules of Play are discussed at length.

Since 1951, the USGA and the R&A have been meeting regularly to establish a uniform code of Rules. *Decisions on the Rules of Golf* is the result of these meetings. Each year, however, brings another round of questions not addressed in the book. Committees meet to discuss these new questions—anything from points of relief from water hazards to playing near a dead snake—and arrive at a decision for each situation. The book is amended every two years.

A *decision* on the Rules has the same status as a Rule and is referenced in *Decisions on the Rules of Golf* by using key words or phrases and a detailed index—the same way you would look up a Rule in the *Rules of Golf.*

As an example, try looking up a few unusual situations involving the flagstick. Unbelievably, there are over 40 decisions under the heading "Flagstick," broken down as subtitles to help you quickly narrow your search. Here are a few examples of situations that really happened, accessed directly from the index:

Question: A player's ball lodges in the flag attached to a flagstick. What is the procedure? **Answer:** A flagstick is a movable obstruction and Rule 24-1 applies. Without penalty, the ball may be placed on the lip of the hole (Decision 17/6).

Question: A player played a stroke from the putting green. The ball struck the hole-liner, which had stuck to the bottom of the flagstick and had come out of the hole when the person attending the flagstick removed the flagstick. Is there a penalty? **Answer:** No. A hole-liner is an outside agency. Accordingly, if the hole-liner was moving when the ball struck it, the stroke is cancelled and the ball must be replaced—Rule 19-1b. If the hole-liner was not moving, the ball must be played as it lies—Rule 19-1. In case of doubt, the ball must be played as it lies (Decision 17/8).

Question: A player holds the flagstick with one hand and holes a short putt, gripping the putter with his other hand. Is this permissible? **Answer:** Yes, provided that the flagstick has been removed from the hole and the ball therefore does not strike it. If the ball were to strike the flagstick, a breach of Rule 17/3a would occur (Decision 17-1/5).

You can obtain a copy of the *Decisions on the Rules of Golf* by contacting the Order Department at the USGA

(908-234-2300), or on the USGA Website (www.usga.org). It makes for interesting reading and you'll find thousands of case studies.

On Correcting Mistakes

Back in the 50's, when Ted Williams and Sam Snead were dominant players, a reporter asked them to compare the difficulty of their respective sports. Williams pointed out that in baseball you use a round bat to hit a round ball traveling close to 100 miles per hour, a ball that sometimes curves, sometimes knuckles and sometimes comes at your head. Snead nodded and said, "Yeah, Ted, but in golf we have to play our foul balls!"

Not all the time. Every golfer has undoubtedly done something on the golf course that he wished he could immediately undo. While some accidents may end up costing you embarrassment, a stroke, or even disqualification, there are times when having a working knowledge of the Rules may save you, because at least some of your mistakes can be corrected—some without penalty.

How many times have you inadvertently knocked your ball off the tee, only to hear someone in your group shout: "That's one!" Well, it's not one. On the teeing ground you are not penalized for accidentally moving your ball, even with a practice swing, unless you've already put the ball *into play* on that hole. Here's where a knowledge of the *Definitions* can really be important.

According to the Rules, a ball is considered to be *in play* only after a player has made a stroke on the teeing ground. A *stroke* is the forward movement of the club made with the *intention* of fairly striking and moving the ball. So, if you *accidentally* move the ball as the result of a practice swing or a nervous twitch, the ball may be replaced without penalty. Don't be lulled into a false sense of security, however: other than on the teeing ground, if you accidentally move your ball in this manner, you must accept a one-stroke penalty and you must replace the ball.

When you drop a ball in the wrong place, or use the wrong dropping technique, or allow another person to drop it for you—all no-nos—you're allowed to correct your mistake without penalty, as long as you correct it before you play your next stroke. The penalties vary if you fail to correct it. The penalty is one stroke if you drop it improperly or have someone else drop it for you, but two strokes if you drop *and play* from the wrong place.

If, in the normal course of play, you damage a club to an extent that it no longer conforms to the Rules, you may replace the club. The same holds true if you arrive at the course with less than the allowable 14 clubs—and there is no penalty, unless you delay play replacing the damaged or missing club.

It is the player's responsibility to turn in an accurate hole-by-hole score. Adding your score correctly, however, is the committee's job. So, it's no problem if you record a wrong score on your card, as long as you correct the error before you return it to the committee. And, even if you were to turn your card in with an addition error, there is no penalty as long as your hole-by-hole scores are correct.

If you accidentally move your opponent's ball or a ball belonging to a fellow competitor while helping in the search for a lost ball, there is no penalty, but the ball must be replaced. Seems only fair, doesn't it? Who would help look otherwise?

If you find yourself confronted with fire ants or in a *dangerous situation* such as a bunker filled with bees, you don't have to risk injury to play the ball. You may, without penalty, drop a ball in the nearest spot that isn't dangerous—but not nearer to the hole. There is one catch, however. If the ball lies in a hazard (which includes a bunker), you must drop the ball in a hazard—and in the same one, if possible. If dropping the ball in the same hazard is not possible, you must drop in a similar, nearby hazard. But in both cases, you can't drop the ball nearer to the hole.

So, use your head, learn the Rules and remember what Yogi Berra said: "90% of the game is half-mental."

✢

Swinging at Mushrooms and Other Rules Conundrums

In what must appear to be the very serious world of the Rules of Golf, there are more humorous incidents than one might believe. Of course, the humor comes only when the incident is re-created, and it is almost always the "victim" who enjoys the retelling the most.

Take, for instance, the guy who thought he had found his ball buried in *the rough*. After a lengthy pre-shot routine—which included a discussion on wind direction and velocity and a club change—his mighty swing resulted in the explosion of a "ball-shaped" mushroom. As if the embarrassment of mistaking a mushroom for a ball wasn't enough, his opponent sprinkled salt on the wound by insisting that since his "intent" was to hit a ball he should lose the hole for playing a *wrong ball*. There was no penalty.

What about the woman who *was* penalized for a lost ball while in the process of taking a *free* drop from ground under repair. This case took place before the rule regarding the dropping procedure had changed. Some may recall that prior to 1984, a drop was properly executed by standing erect, facing the hole and dropping the ball over your shoulder. The woman followed the procedure to the letter, but when she turned to check her lie, she couldn't find her ball. Her entire group joined the futile search before concluding that she had to proceed under the lost ball rule.

The mystery wasn't solved until the woman stopped by the golf shop to tell her tale to a golf professional. As she demonstrated the drop, the pro noticed that she was wearing a hooded windbreaker. "Elementary, Mrs. Watson," the pro proclaimed, as he pulled the ball out of her hood. "The ball never touched the ground."

An incident whose details can only improve with age occurred at the Apawamis Club in Rye, New York, at a United States Senior Golf Association Championship. A roving rules official observed two competitors engaged in an animated discussion on the apron of the ninth green. A ball had landed on a wad of bubble gum and, when it came to rest, the gum was securely attached. The player felt that he should be entitled to remove the gum, but a fellow competitor insisted that he was not allowed to "clean" the ball until it was on the green.

The answer? Chewing gum is artificial and therefore is defined as an *obstruction* and, given its size and weight, it would further be classified as a *movable* obstruction. Anywhere on the course, relief from interference by movable obstructions such as paper cups or soda cans is gained by *moving the obstruction*. However, if the ball lies in or on the obstruction, the ball may be lifted and cleaned without penalty.

This is very different from having a *loose impediment*—natural things such as leaves, sand or mud—adhere to your ball. If a loose impediment adheres to your ball, you are not permitted to remove it until it comes to rest on the putting green.

Finally, a chuckle came via a phone call on a cool November morning. "What temperature does it have to be to play winter rules?"

Order of Play

For many of us, our first lesson on the Rules of Golf may have occurred before our very first shot. I can still remember walking up to the first tee on caddie day, only to be told, "Hold it right there, you don't have the honor."

Rule 10 (Order of Play) seems pretty straightforward, but violations can be awkward and some may remember an international "incident" that occurred during a Solheim Cup match in 2000 when Annika Sorenstam chipped in for birdie—before her opponent had attempted her long birdie putt—then was challenged as to whether it had been her turn to play. The incident? Some felt her opponent was guilty of poor sportsmanship for standing by while Sorenstam played out of turn, then speaking up *to cancel her shot* only *after* her great chip. According to the Rules, however, her opponent was correct in doing so.

Here's the way Rule 10 reads: "The player to play first is said to have the 'honor.'" The honor on the first tee is determined by a draw. In the absence of a draw the honor should be determined by lot—as through flipping a coin or tee.

The side that wins a hole in match play or has the lowest score in stroke play shall take the honor at the next teeing ground. If a hole has been halved or stroke play competitors have the same score, they should play from the tee in the same order as on the previous teeing ground.

When the balls are *in play*, the ball farthest from the hole shall be played first. If the balls are equidistant from the hole, the order of play shall be determined by lot.

Balls belonging to the same side may be played in the order the side considers best (Rule 30-3c).

As basic as this Rule may seem in writing, it often causes problems, particularly with different formats and types of events. Here are some examples and common questions:

If Player A is on the green 40 feet from the hole and Player B is in a bunker but only 30 feet from the hole, who has the honor? Player A. It makes no difference whether a ball is on the green or not, the player whose ball is farthest from the hole has the honor.

Players A and B are both on the green and their balls appear to be the exact same distance from the hole. How do you determine the honor? It really doesn't happen often, but during the 2000 U.S. Amateur at Baltusrol Jerry Courville, Jr., and James Driscoll *both* hit balls to within 18 to 20 feet of the hole. Veteran Rules Official Joe Cantwell was the referee and could not determine the honor by eye so he pulled out a spool of string to measure the distances. It turned out that they were equidistant. He then reached into his pocket for a coin but discovered he did not have one so he borrowed a coin from one of the players and flipped it to determine the honor. This may seem like an odd procedure, but Mr. Cantwell had proceeded "by the book."

Who plays first when both players lift their balls to take relief from *ground under repair* (GUR) or the same water hazard? The honor would go to the player whose ball was farthest from the hole *before* it was lifted from the GUR or retrieved from the water hazard. If two balls are hit into and *lost* in the same water hazard, the honor would be determined by "lot," such as a flip of the coin.

How do you determine the honor in a handicap event? In match play, the winner of the hole has the honor so the *net* score would be used to determine the honor. In stroke play, when the handicap is deducted at the end of the round and not on individual holes, the gross score would be used to determine the honor on the next tee. An exception to this would be four-ball stroke play where the honor would be determined by the low net score.

In four-ball, can you allow your partner to knock in a short putt if you have the honor, even if he's "inside" your opponents? Yes. The side with the honor may play in the order the side considers best.

Can a player choose to putt out rather than mark and lift his ball? Yes and no. In stroke play, it can speed up play so the practice is not discouraged. In match play, there is no such option.

What happens if a player plays out of turn? In stroke play, there is no penalty unless the committee determines that the competitors have agreed to play out of order to give one of them an advantage. In match play, there is no penalty either; however, the opponent may require the player to cancel the stroke and play a ball in correct order, as was the case with Annika.

You can usually avoid needless penalties—and criticism—by being aware of who's "away" and improve your pace of play by being ready to play when you have the honor.

Two Different Games

I believe every golfer who makes an effort to learn more about the Rules enjoys the game a little more. An understanding of the Rules brings with it more of an appreciation for the history of golf and a respect for the game's nuances, its language and its traditions.

All of us in the business of teaching the Rules acknowledge that by design or neglect, accurately or not, golf's TV announcers impart information about the Rules of Golf to more golfers during one telecast than we'll impact in a year—maybe a lifetime! Perhaps this is why I hold my breath before every two-man sudden death tour playoff when announcers say, or imply, a common misconception by announcing that "this is match play—this is not medal play!" What they really mean is that the players' strategy would be *more like match play* since each would now only have one man to beat.

The major difference between match and stroke play is that in match play you play against an opponent and the game is played by holes—which you win, lose or halve—and violations of general rules result in the loss of a hole. In stroke play, the field comprises fellow competitors. The winner has the fewest number of strokes, and violations of the same general rules would result in a two-stroke penalty—but there are other differences:

- If I tee up and play my ball from outside the teeing ground in stroke play, I incur a two-stroke penalty and I must replay the stroke from within the teeing ground (before teeing off on the next hole) or be disqualified (Rule 11). In match play, there is no penalty for the same violation. My opponent, however, would have the option of either letting my stroke count or requiring me to do it all over again, without penalty, but from the right place.

- In stroke play, I am penalized two strokes if my putt strikes another ball lying on the putting green. Once again, in match play there is no penalty, even if my putt strikes my opponent's or partner's ball. However, in order to keep me from using any other ball as a backstop or otherwise gaining an advantage in a match, my opponent(s) could require me to have any (or all) other balls marked and lifted before I putt—and I must oblige (Rule 22).

- In match play, I can concede my opponent's next stroke, the hole or even the match (Rule 2-4). In stroke play, everyone must "hole out" on every hole or suffer disqualification.

- Unless a referee has been assigned to your match, you—and only you—can *call the hole* or make a *claim* if you notice your opponent breaking a rule. Your claim however, must be made before either you or your opponent tee off on the next hole, or you lose your right to call the hole. In stroke play, there is no such "statute of limitations" until the competition has closed: Anyone, not just a fellow competitor, can bring a violation to the attention of the committee, who can then assess a penalty—which has led to a number of controversial viewer "call-in" penalties and disqualifications.

Match and stroke play are two different games with different Rules. Those who know the differences may enjoy and appreciate the game just a little bit more—and they may have earned a little advantage as well.

❧

Making Claims

When it comes to calling penalties in match play I often relate it to a two-on-two pick-up basketball game. It's not a foul unless you call it!

In match play, if a dispute arises between the players, a player may make a *claim*, as described earlier. If the claim is immediately lodged directly to a member of the committee, a decision should be made as quickly as possible. If no one on the committee is available, the players must *continue the match without delay*.

According to Rule 2-5, the committee may consider a claim only if the player making the claim notifies his opponent: (i) that he is making a claim; (ii) of the facts of the situation; and (iii) that he wants a ruling. In addition, the claim must be made before any player in the match plays from the next tee or in the case of the last hole of the match, before all players in the match leave the putting green.

Here is an example. While playing the fourth hole, your opponent's ball ends up on an area of "hardpan" just off the fairway. He insists that he is entitled to *free* relief and you disagree. Since there is no one around to make an immediate ruling, the Rules require you to continue play. So, your opponent takes relief by lifting and dropping his ball—as if the hardpan were *ground under repair*. You are now faced with the decision to accept the fact that he got to move his ball off the bad lie or make a claim.

In order to make a *valid* claim, you must inform your opponent that you are making a claim (speak up). You must spell out what you are claiming (free relief from hardpan in the rough is not permitted) and announce that you'd like the Rules of Golf applied. Simply saying, "that doesn't seem fair" or "are you sure" does not constitute a claim.

In order for the claim to be *timely* you must make it before either of you hit from the fifth tee. So, it's too late to make a valid claim "at the turn" when a friend tells you that you could have "called the hole" or on the back nine, when your opponent denies you relief from a similar condition.

Any later claim should *not* be considered unless it is based on facts you were previously *unaware of* and you had been given wrong information by your opponent. Back to our example. Let's say you were unaware that your opponent took relief from the hardpan because you were off looking for your own ball. And, when he announced his score for the hole, he did not include a penalty for having moved his ball. If, before the results of the match were officially announced, you became aware that he simply took relief without your knowledge and told you he "made a 3" on the hole you could still make a valid claim.

Once the results of the match have been officially announced, a later claim may not be considered unless the committee is satisfied that your opponent *knew* he was giving you wrong information. By the way, it is the player's responsibility to know the Rules, and a player is deemed to have given *wrong information* even if it is due to the failure to include a penalty that he did not know that he had incurred.

When Rules Stymie….or "Doubt as to Procedure"
Keeping in mind Yogi Berra's sage advice, "It ain't over 'til it's over," my comment regarding Ken Venturi's regular assertions that Arnold Palmer got away with a Rules violation during the 1958 Masters would be: "Ken, it's over!"

While Venturi agreed that Arnie *should* have been granted relief for an embedded ball behind Augusta's famed par-3

12th hole, the Rules official did not. According to Ken, after hitting a poor chip shot, Arnie *then* decided to play a second ball. Ken knew you must announce your intention to play a second ball *before* you hit the first and disagreed with the Committee's decision to allow the score with the second ball to count. This saved the "King" two pivotal strokes toward his first "Green Jacket".

Venturi's claim, more than a half-decade after the incident, did bring Rule 3-3 (Doubt as to Procedure) front and center and may be worth a review.

Rule 3-3 is too often confused with a provisional ball (Rule 25-2) that may only be used when you believe your ball might have gone out of bounds or be lost outside a water hazard. Rule 3-3 allows a player who finds himself in a situation where he is unsure of his rights to play a *second ball*.

Given the fact that you will actually have two balls in play simultaneously, there are two very important preconditions that must be met before implementing this "second-ball Rule." First, you must announce your intention to invoke Rule 3-3, and second, you must specify which of the two balls you want to count if the Rules permit.

Here's an example. You hit a perfect drive only to discover that your ball came to rest in a deep tire rut created by a gang mower. You feel you should be entitled to relief but you're not sure which rule applies. Before taking a stroke or lifting the ball to take relief, you must inform a member of your group that you are invoking Rule 3-3 and will play a *second ball*. You must also announce that if the committee determines that you *are* entitled to relief, you want your score with the second ball to count.

It is important to emphasize that these announcements must take place *before* you take any action. You cannot wait and see if you hit a good or bad shot from the original lie. Back to our example... Let's say you miraculously knock your ball onto the green from the rutted lie. At this point, you might be tempted to forget about playing a second ball and simply continue play with your original ball. That would be a mistake. Once you announce your intention to apply Rule 3-3, you must follow through and play out the hole with both balls or risk disqualification.

So, after playing the original ball, you would then drop another ball no closer to the hole and within a club length of the *nearest point of relief* and play out the hole with both balls.

Let's say you score a par 4 with the original ball, the one you played from the rutted lie, and bogey 5 with the second ball. When your round is complete you would report all the facts to the committee, which would then decide if you should have been entitled to relief.

If they rule that the tire rut constituted *ground under repair*, you would count the score you made with the second ball—the one you took relief with—even though it happened to be the higher score. On the other hand, if the committee decided that you were not entitled to relief, you would count the score you made with your original ball.

One final point: Rule 3-3 logically *cannot* be used in match play since your opponent's strategy, as well as your own, is almost always based on the current state of the match.

Member-Guest & Club Competitions: When Rules Tensions Flare

Although the golf season runs year-round, the volume of Rules questions has its peaks and valleys. One of the peaks comes around Labor Day when a majority of clubs conducts their annual club championships. The other is July and August, when every club seems to schedule a major member-guest.

While most of us profess to playing U.S. Golf Association rules all the time, we don't always live and play by the letter of the law. This all changes, of course, when the bell rings for the big events of the summer—member-guests and club championships.

I've played in a few of those three-day, round-robin match-play member-guests and although I try to remain anonymous, I occasionally get called on to answer questions on the Rules, sometimes after the fact, often in the clubhouse or from an adjacent fairway.

Here's a sampling of a few situations that have come up:

After playing four holes, one of the players on Team A—which had lost holes one and two, tied the third and lost the fourth—discovered he had started the match with 15 clubs.

Question One: The partner with the extra club had played poorly and had not figured in on the result of any hole. Did that relieve the team of the penalty? No, it did not. Rule 30-3e says the *side* shall be penalized for a breach of Rule 4-4 (maximum of 14 clubs) by any partner—so you may want to check your partner's bag as well as your own on the first tee.

Question Two: The players knew the penalty would be the loss of a hole, with a maximum penalty of two holes, but since Team A lost the first and second holes, anyway, in effect there would be no penalty, right? Rule 4-4 reads: "At the conclusion of the hole at which the breach is discovered, the *state of the match* shall be adjusted by deducting one hole for each hole at which the breach occurred. Maximum deduction per round: two holes." As Team A stood three down after four holes, they became five down after four holes, once the penalty was applied!

In the grill after a round, a player asked me how the Rules applied if he played a provisional ball and hit into the same general area as his original tee shot, he finds both, but can't tell one ball from the other. Seasoned players wouldn't think of putting a ball into play without a personal identification mark on it, but weekend players often fail to do this. Actually, this player was not the first to face this situation and there is a relevant decision (Decision 27/11). This is one of the few times a player can take his pick and play either ball—but it will cost him since he lies three, whichever ball he picks.

Our afternoon match was against a team that warned us to watch out when we played the team—and their great caddie—that had just beaten them. It seems the caddie read greens beautifully. Knowing he could not touch the green to point out the line of putt, they had devised a system in which the caddie would tend the flagstick and stand so that his right foot would indicate the line. The system worked like a charm and our opponents were anxious to try it themselves—against us! I told them that Rule 8-2 (Indicating Line of Play) and Decision 8-2b/1 that deals with a caddie using his shadow for the identical purpose, would prevent them from utilizing this "system."

The talk of the weekend, though, involved the hole location on the 18th. The superintendent had the greens rolling very fast, at close to 11 on the Stimpmeter, and the committee opted to use a front-right hole location. When the greens are at their usual 9.5 speed, this hole location is very challenging. This time, the location was just plain silly. Player after player watched in agony as balls rolled up to the hole, peeked in, then rolled back down the hill. One group actually agreed to a halved hole after all four players had taken four putts each, and no one had holed out!

After viewing the carnage from the 18th fairway, one team decided to test the committee and the Rules. One at a time, they stroked their putts, then followed the ball up the hill and tapped the ball into the hole from short range, just as it began its retreat down the hill—willing to accept a two-stroke penalty under Rule 14-5 (Playing a moving ball). Given the humorous nature of the hole location, their strategy may have been solid—but their knowledge of the Rules was not. A two-stroke penalty would apply only in stroke play. In match play, the penalty is loss of hole, which handed the hole to their bewildered but grateful opponents.

Local Rules

When we tee it up for casual play there is commonly an unspoken agreement to play by USGA Rules. Differing levels of interest in, understanding of and respect for, the Rules result in countless misapplications, disputes, arguments and Rules calls to the USGA.

At every level of competitive golf—from a country club scramble to the U.S. Open—there is a committee responsible for laying down the conditions under which the competition is to be played.

Some committees take their responsibility a little more seriously than others do but each is responsible, under the Rules, for laying down the conditions under which the competition is to be played. The committee is also responsible for settling disputes, defining the boundaries of the course and the margins of the hazards, suspending or canceling play due to inclement weather and announcing the starting times and pairings.

The committee does not have the authority to waive a rule of golf, but they do have the power to make and the responsibility to publish any *local rules*.

Some local rules are used so often that we often mistakenly think of them as Rules of Golf. For example, the local rule granting relief for an embedded ball *through the green* and the local rule defining areas such as turf nurseries and newly planted trees as *ground under repair* are good examples. It is important to remember that these are *not* Rules of Golf but rather conditions used at the discretion of the committee.

Other local rules are rarely, if ever, used at the club level but, because they are always in effect for PGA Tour events, they tend to cause confusion. For instance, the Tours have used local rules prohibiting a player from changing the type of ball he is playing during a round (the "one-ball rule") and, at one time, required a player to use a small coin placed directly behind his ball when marking the position of his ball. Another local rule prohibits practice putting or chipping on or near the putting green of the hole last played.

Lacking these local rules, you and I are free to change from one brand, compression or type of ball to another between holes as many times as we wish; mark the position of our ball with a tee (or even the toe of our putter) and, as long as we do not delay play, we can practice putting after holing out.

A while back, the USGA/R&A approved language for a local rule giving the *Committee* the authority to allow the use of electronic measuring devices, and another to treat stones in bunkers as movable obstructions and to grant line-of-play relief from fixed sprinkler caps (when the cap is located within two club lengths of the green and your ball lies within two club lengths of the cap).

Don't be caught unaware. Always carry a Rules book in your bag, and check for any local rules in effect at the course you play.

PART TWO

From Tee to Green

Begin at the Beginning

PGA PROFESSIONALS OFTEN REMIND US OF THE VALUE of a pre-shot routine—and they're right. A pre-round routine wouldn't hurt either because, in addition to the nervous jokes and last-second swing search, some say the first tee is where matches are often won or lost!

It's also where the game begins, and it's where you should take time to organize your thoughts and check your equipment as you prepare to do battle.

Before stepping onto the tee, count your clubs, because once you've put a ball into play you'll earn a penalty if it turns out you began play with more than 14 clubs. The penalty? You must adjust the status of a match by deducting one hole for each hole on which you were in violation of Rule 4-4 (up to a maximum of two holes).

In stroke play, you are penalized two strokes for every hole you play with too many clubs, up to a maximum of four strokes, and the penalty should be assessed by adding two strokes to your score for each of the first two holes. The penalty for carrying too many clubs is heavy. So, count carefully. It can happen, as it did, to Ian Woosman at the British Open!

Once you've discovered you started the round with more than 14 clubs, you must immediately reduce your arsenal to 14. Don't make the mistake of continuing play with the excess clubs under the logic that you were already assessed the maximum penalty! If you did continue play, without taking the excess club(s) out of play, you would be disqualified! By the way, you can take the extra club out of play by simply identifying the excess club—and not using it again. You do not need to physically abandon the club or break it into pieces!

Before your first tee shot you should also put a distinguishing mark on your ball. Even if the rest of your group plays different brands and numbers, if any situation arises in which you can't positively identify a ball as your own, you are deemed to have lost your ball! Marking your ball also lowers the risk of hitting a wrong ball, or another golfer accidentally hitting your ball.

This is also the time to convert your Handicap Index to a Course Handicap for the course and tees you're about to play. If you carelessly declare a course handicap higher than you are entitled to, the penalty is disqualification.

When it is your turn to play, remember that the teeing ground is a rectangular area that extends two club-lengths back from the outside, front edge of the tee-markers. Your ball must be played from this area, but there is no requirement that you take your stance within this *teeing ground*. Please note that despite the popularity of the expression "tee-box," the correct term is "teeing ground": you won't find tee-box in the Rules book.

Interestingly, tee-markers, on the hole you are playing, have a kind of chameleon-like quality to them. Until you put a ball into play they're deemed to be fixed and may not be moved. But if you hit a wild tee shot or flub one so badly that it comes to rest where any tee-marker interferes with your lie, stance, line of play or area of intended swing, you are free to move the marker. Just be sure to return the tee-marker to its original position after you play.

As play begins, the *honor* or *order of play*, as described earlier, is determined by lot, unless pairings have been announced, which would mean that the side listed first has the honor. The honor on subsequent holes goes to the side that won the preceding hole. If the hole was halved, the side that had the honor on the preceding tee retains it. If the net score on the hole determines the result, then it is the net score that determines the honor.

In stroke play, there's no penalty for playing out of order unless the committee determines that players agreed to do so to give one or both of them an advantage. All players party to such an agreement would be disqualified! In match play there is no penalty, but a player may immediately require his opponent to cancel his stroke and play again, in the correct order.

Arriving at the *starting point* late will cost you. In most cases, the starting point is the first tee, but there are occasions when you might be assigned to start on number 10 for a two-tee start or some other hole for a "shotgun start." If you miss your time, but do manage to get to the tee within five minutes of your assigned time, the penalty, in stroke play, is two strokes. In match play, you've lost the first hole. If you arrive more than five minutes after your assigned time, the penalty is disqualification, in both stroke play and match play.

In four-ball play, a side can proceed, without penalty, even if one of the partners is missing. The latecomer can join the match—but only between holes. You may want to remind him to set the alarm for the next time he's your partner!

Addressing the Ball

How many remember the *Honeymooners* classic when Ed Norton helped Ralph Kramden learn the game overnight so that the big-mouth could keep a golf game with his boss.

Conducted in Ralph's tiny kitchen, but only after the purchase of a gaudy golf outfit, the first lesson began at the tee. "Address the ball," Norton directed and Ralph's historic response: "Hello, ball!"

Ralph's outing was a predictable disaster, but you can avoid needless penalties by knowing the dos and don'ts associated with addressing the ball.

A player has *addressed the ball* once he has grounded his club—either immediately in front of or immediately behind his ball. It is important to understand exactly when you have addressed the ball. Once a ball *in play* is addressed, you will incur a penalty stroke and be required to replace the ball if the ball moves for *any* reason—unless it is "known" or "virtually certain" that the player did not cause the ball to move (Rule 18-2b). However, on the teeing ground, there is no penalty if a ball moves inadvertently at address.

Despite Norton's directive, there is no requirement that a player address the ball prior to taking a stroke. In fact, many great players avoid grounding their club prior to the stroke and therefore never address their ball. All-time great Jack Nicklaus held his club just off the ground as he prepared to play a stroke. I've heard golfers say that by following this procedure Jack eliminates the possibility of a penalty should his ball move before he played. This is *close* to true. But consider this question submitted to the USGA: "A player took several practice swings about one foot from his ball and his club came in contact with the ground. He then took his stance, touched the light rough behind the ball with his clubhead but did not ground the club. At that point the ball moved."

The player claimed that no penalty was incurred, because he had not addressed the ball. However, the Committee judged that the practice swings and the touching of the grass behind the ball may have caused the ball to move, and therefore the player incurred a penalty stroke under Rule 18-2a. Was the committee correct?"

The USGA (Decision 18-2a/30) explained that it is a question of fact whether the player caused his ball to move. If he did, he would incur a penalty under Rule 18-2a (Ball Moved by Player, Partner, Caddie or Equipment). At times, though, there is a *presumption of guilt* and the USGA reasoned that because of the practice swings and touching of the grass, the weight of evidence is against the player and concluded that the player had caused his ball to move and therefore upheld the committee's decision.

When a ball in play *moves*, the player will not be excused from penalty simply because he has not addressed his ball and, therefore, must exercise caution whenever he (or his caddie or partner) is in the vicinity of his ball. Players should take extra care when their ball comes to rest in a heavily wooded area, thick rough or a dry water hazard. A player who approaches his ball, even without a club, even to identify his ball or to determine how he wishes to play his next shot, would be subject to penalty if he caused the ball to move. Remember that there may be a *presumption of guilt* if your ball moves and you've been anywhere near it, so be very careful every time you approach your ball and take your stance. The fact that you have not addressed the ball may relieve you of penalty under 18-2b, but your very presence in the vicinity of your ball might be deemed to have caused the ball to move and lead to a penalty under Rule 18-2a.

What's a Backswing; What's a Stroke?

Talk to any golf professional about the importance of a smooth, one-piece backswing and he'll talk chapter and verse. Read the *Rules of Golf* and you'll find that a *stroke* is the *forward* movement of the club made with the *intention* of fairly striking at and moving the ball. In other words, according to the USGA, the backswing is *not* a part of a stroke!

On those few occasions when your ball is inside the margin of a water hazard, but still playable, it is not unusual to find loose impediments in the proximity of the ball. And, while you are not permitted to move or touch a loose impediment when your ball and the loose impediment are both in the hazard, it might be possible to play a stroke despite some interference with loose impediments. When you understand that there is NO penalty if you touch or move a loose impediment *during your stroke* AND that the stroke is the "forward movement of the club," you can understand why experienced players may not shy away from playing a ball out of a water hazard. But be sure to take extra care not to touch any loose impediments, such as leaves or twigs, during your backswing.

Some may recall a virtual Rules "seminar" on this very subject that occurred at the Harbour Town Golf Links during the Verizon Heritage Championship when Brian Davis incurred a two-stroke penalty that sealed his fate during a playoff with Jim Furyk. His mistake? He touched a loose impediment in a hazard prior to his stroke! The TV announcers correctly quoted Rule 13-4, but misunderstood the definition of a *stroke*, for while it is okay to touch a loose impediment during the *stroke*, Brian touched it on his backswing. Adding to the confusion was the fact that Davis touched what some interpreted as a live, rooted plant when, in fact, it was detached and, therefore, defined as a loose impediment.

Out of Bounds: Not So Simple

"Out of Bounds" is covered under Rule 27 along with Lost

and Provisional Balls. One of the most concisely written of the 34 Rules might imply simplicity. Think again. The staggering total of 75 Decisions on Out of Bounds alone suggests that the Rule has some hidden intricacies.

Out of Bounds is ground from which a ball may *not* be played and you may find the boundaries of a course marked in many different ways. No matter how it's marked, your ball is not "out" unless the *entire* ball lies out of bounds.

The most common method to indicate out of bounds is the use of fence posts or white stakes. When used, the nearest *inside* points at *ground level*, excepting angled supports, define out of bounds. Any part of an angled support or guide wire that is *in* bounds is an immovable obstruction, so you would be entitled to relief without penalty (Decision 24/2). On the other hand, a concrete base supporting a boundary fence post—or a part of the OB fence that is bowed or curled towards the course—are *not* obstructions. So, there is no *free relief* (D24/3 and D24/4).

There may be times when the course staff or the committee in charge of a competition finds it necessary or desirable to connect OB stakes with a white line on the ground. When used, the line takes precedence over the stakes and the line itself is out of bounds.

Whether a ball is "in" or "out" depends on where the ball *comes to rest*. If you sliced one onto an adjacent interstate highway and the ball rebounds off an 18-wheeler back onto the course you are *in* bounds. If your ball bounces off a green-high cart path and goes OB you are *out*. Similarly, if your ball enters a water hazard and is carried OB by the current it's OB. However, if the current brings it back from OB you are *in*. Luck goes both ways.

One more specific to remember: if you hit a ball that might be OB, the Rules permit you to play a *provisional ball*. In order to take advantage of this time-saving courtesy, you must announce your intention to play a provisional, and you must play the provisional *before* you go forward to search for your wayward shot. Decision 27-2a/1 makes it very clear that your announcement must be specific. You must get the words "provisional ball" into your announcement. Comments like, "that might be out of here," or "I'd better hit another one" are not sufficient since they could be interpreted to mean you are simply putting another ball into play.

When You Are Lost and When You Are Not

When is a lost ball not a *lost ball*? Most golfers know that according to the Rules, a ball is lost if it is neither found nor identified within five minutes of when the player, his partner or their caddies begin to search for it.

The Rules say that when a ball is lost, the player has only one option—commonly called *stroke and distance*. He must accept a one-stroke penalty and give up the distance his last stroke traveled by, "playing a ball from as near as possible to the spot from which his previous stroke was played."

Sounds simple enough doesn't it? But hold on. As strange as it may sound, there are times when a ball that can't be found is not a lost ball and times when you may actually find your ball and yet it still will be considered lost!

It's easier to deal with the second situation first. Let's say you hit a drive into a trouble area, take a quick look then return to the tee and play another ball while the rest of your group continues the search. Following this sequence, your second drive becomes your *ball in play* as soon as you make a stroke at it, while your original ball—even if it is found within the five minutes allowed by the Rules—will be considered a lost ball.

The mistake many golfers make is thinking that by returning to the tee to play a second ball they are playing a provisional. They aren't. A provisional ball must be announced and played *before* you go forward to search for your first ball.

Now let's say you pull-top your drive into some bushes then, in a pique of rage, blast a prodigious provisional down the middle. You send your caddie into the bush in search for the mis-hit, grab your 3-metal and storm after your well-hit provisional. Just *after* you hit a second shot with the provisional, but well within the five-minute limit, your caddie finds your first ball.

Forget it! Once you play a second stroke with the provisional from a point nearer to the hole than the original ball was likely to have been, your original was *deemed* lost.

Now, for some good news—examples of when a ball that is lost *isn't* a lost ball.

Each example depends on it being *known or being virtually certain* that a ball has been lost under certain conditions. ("Known or virtually certain" is not sharply defined in the Rules, so that sensible judgments can be made using all available evidence and according to the specific situation.)

Let's say that you hit your ball directly toward a large pond marked as a water hazard but—short of diving to the bottom to retrieve it—you can't prove for certain that your ball found a watery grave. If it is known or virtually certain that the ball came to rest in the water hazard, then it is not considered a lost ball. While it will still cost you a penalty stroke, at least you'll have options in addition to stroke-and-distance.

Even better—and often overlooked—if it is known or virtually certain that your ball is lost in casual water or in an area marked as ground under repair, in a burrowing animal hole or an immovable obstruction (*through the green*), you are entitled to relief *without* penalty. The relief procedure can be tricky, however, because for the purpose of applying these Rules, the ball shall be deemed to lie at the spot where it last crossed the margin of these abnormal ground conditions or where it entered the obstruction.

Finally, if it is known or virtually certain that a ball was taken by an outside agency, a player in another group perhaps, or a dog roaming the course, it is not a lost ball. Without penalty, another ball must be placed on the spot from which the original was moved. Of course it is likely that you will not know the *exact* spot it was moved from, so a ball should be dropped as near as possible to the place from which your group estimates the ball was taken.

Losing a Golf Ball...by the Book

Has this ever happened to you? You try to bust a drive to put yourself into position to reach a par 5 in two, but you pull-hook it instead...deep into the woods. You reach into your pocket for another ball and announce through clenched teeth that you're going to hit a provisional, then proceed to pound a perfect drive right down the middle.

As you wade into the thicket to begin searching for your original ball, thoughts suddenly occur to you. *Why am I searching for this ball, anyway? If I find it, and try to play it, it'll probably take two or three shots just to hack it back to the fairway. If I find it and it's unplayable, my only viable option will be to return to the tee playing three, in which case I'd have to match that great provisional. I* do not *want to find this ball!*

After a quick look, you announce to the group: "Forget it, that one's lost, I'm going to play the other ball," and stalk out of the woods. However, before you can play your next shot, one of your opponents decides that he'll do you a favor and continue the search and, just before the five-minute limit expires, he finds a ball that he's pretty sure is yours...nestled, of course, under a thick bush.

Was your declaration that "the ball is lost" binding? Are you actually obligated to search for your ball? And what happens if, like the proverbial bad penny, the original ball is found but you'd rather play the provisional?

According to Rule 27, a ball is considered lost if: the player who hit it neither finds it nor identifies it as his own within five minutes after the player's side (his partner(s) and their caddies) have begun to search for it; the player has put another ball into play; or the player has played any stroke with a substituted ball or with a provisional ball from the place where the original ball is likely to be, or from a point nearer to the hole than that spot.

"Declaring" a ball lost is meaningless, but there is also nothing in the Rules that requires a player to search for a potentially lost ball. In fact, if you simply play another ball after hitting a poor drive—without announcing your intention to play a provisional—the first ball *is* considered lost.

In the circumstances described earlier, it might have been smart to do just that. The trouble is, you must decide *before* you begin your search whether your second play from the tee is a provisional or if you are putting another ball into play and hitting three. And since you don't know if your second effort is going to be perfect, much less any better than the first one, you're almost always better off declaring your second shot from the tee to be a provisional. Remember, if you put another ball into play rather than play a provisional, you give up the option of playing the original ball, which may have looked real bad on the way into the woods, but just might end up in a playable position.

But what about the do-gooder who ends up finding a ball that might be yours? Can you ignore him if you don't want to find the original and want only to accept the penalty and play on with your provisional? Unfortunately, no. Decision 27-2c/2 states that a player is obligated to inspect the ball that has been found and, if it turns out to be his, he must abandon the provisional ball and continue play with the original—or proceed under the unplayable ball rule.

Let's go back and take a quick look at Rule 27. "A ball is considered 'lost' if a player plays any stroke with a provisional from a place nearer to the hole than the original was likely to be." Okay, suppose I block my tee shot on a par 3 deep into the woods, then announce and play a provisional that I knock to within inches of the hole. Can my opponent insist on searching for my first ball, or can I ignore him and go directly to the green and tap in the provisional for a four?

The answer is *both*. If my opponent finds my original ball before I tap in the provisional, I'm obligated to play the original. But if I tap in the provisional before he finds the original ball, the provisional becomes the ball in play, even if I had putted out of turn. In that case, he could require me to replay the stroke in the correct order, but there would be no penalty and the provisional ball would be the ball in play (Decision 27-2b/1).

It's not too difficult to imagine a rather comical foot race between two determined opponents, one sprinting toward the green, putter in hand, and the other scrambling into the woods in a frenzied search for the errant shot.

Improving Your Stance or Swing

Rule 13-2 says that *through the green* a player shall not improve his: (1) lie, (2) stance, (3) area of his intended swing, (4) line of play, or (5) area in which he is to drop his ball by: (i) pressing a club on the ground; (ii) moving, bending or breaking anything growing or fixed; (iii) creating or eliminating irregularities of the surface; (iv) removing or pressing down sand, loose soil, replaced divots, dew, frost or water! Play the ball as it lies!

There are some logical exceptions. You may (1) lightly ground your club while addressing the ball, (2) "fairly" take your stance and (3) during the backswing of a *completed* stroke. There is no penalty if you break off a leaf or branch on your backswing as long *as you complete your stroke.* Another exception to Rule 13-2, however, says that in *making a stroke*—or during the backward movement of your club for a stroke (your backswing) if you were to break a branch, knock off a few leaves or cut down some fescue grass—there is no penalty, *as long as you complete your swing!* If you did improve the area of your swing on your backswing—but for some reason *aborted the swing*—you would be slapped with a two-stroke penalty under Rule 13-2.

The use of the word "fairly" is intended to *require* the player to take the *least intrusive* manner that results in the *minimum improvement* in the area of his intended stance, swing or line of play. The player does not have a right nor is he "entitled" to a normal stance or swing. He must accommodate the situation and take a stance as normal as circumstances permit.

Even when your ball is not in big trouble and not in a hazard—referred to as *through the green*—you are not permitted to do anything that would improve the position of your ball or the area of your intended swing. This means you may not step behind your ball to press down the ground and improve your lie, use your club like a sickle to clear away high grass near your ball or clear your swing path by removing branches or leaves by hand—or with a *practice* swing.

Here are a few of the most common questions I've fielded over the years on improving your stance or the area of your intended swing...

Question: If a player breaks a branch during a swing there is no penalty. If he improves the area of his intended swing with a "practice" swing he is penalized. What if a player stops his swing after breaking an impeding branch on his backswing?

Answer: He incurs a two-stroke penalty or loss of hole in match play. (Decision 13-2/14.5)

Question: A player knocks down a single leaf with a practice swing. Should he be penalized?

Answer: You'd have to be there to answer this one. Simply knocking down a leaf on a practice swing is not a penalty. It becomes a penalty when the removal of that leaf "improves the area of his intended swing." In some cases it might, in another situation knocking down several leaves may not! (Decision 13-2/22)

Question: During a practice swing an interfering branch is broken. To avoid a penalty, the player decides to play in another direction so that the area of his swing will not be improved by the breaking of the branch. Is he still subject to penalty?

Answer: Yes. The player was in breach of Rule 13-2 as soon as he improved the area of the originally intended swing. (Decision 13/2/24)

Marking the Ball

An "X" marked the spot where the legendary treasure of Long John Silver was buried and, believe it or not, it would also suffice when marking the position of your ball on a putting green.

When your ball is on the putting green, you are permitted to lift it in order to clean it, bless it, or just to get it out of the way while other players putt. The Rules say that the ball must be marked *before* it is lifted, but aside from a subtle recommendation following Rule 20-1, there is nothing to tell you how to mark it.

For instance, short of a local rule used by some professional tours, there is nothing in the Rules that requires you to mark your ball by placing a small coin or ball marker (as Rule 20 recommends) directly behind the ball. However, there are decisions on the Rules, which have been made and published, that could make disregarding this customary procedure costly.

You may, for instance, scratch a line on the green to "mark the spot," but you run the risk of being accused of testing the putting surface or of indicating a line for your putt. Both involve penalties. Marking your ball with a leaf or flower petal also is permitted, but this is inadvisable since the mark might easily be moved by the draft of a passing player or a puff of wind. And, using the toe of your putter may be convenient and within the Rules, but it's not a good habit to get into.

Whether a golfer marks his ball on the green with a coin, a tee, or even a pebble, the player about to putt can ask for the mark to be moved to one side or the other if he feels it would interfere with his putt, his field of vision, or even his concentration. Once asked, the player must oblige or be penalized (in stroke play the player required to lift could putt out first rather than mark his ball). This was not the case in match play as recently as the early 80's when the player who had the honor "controlled" all the balls on the putting green and could use his partner's or opponent's ball to his advantage (such as using it as a backstop on a down-hill putt). All this changed in 1984 and no longer is anyone required to leave his ball on the green to the advantage of an opponent. In fact, any player may have any ball lifted, at any time, if he feels it may interfere with or assist another player.

If the mark, or the ball, is accidentally moved, and the movement is directly attributable to the process of marking the position of or the lifting of the ball, the ball must be replaced, without penalty. This would apply even if the coin you used to mark your ball had, to your surprise, stuck to the sole of your putter when you attempted to press it down.

On Replacing the Ball

Replacing a lifted ball means returning it to the exact spot from which it was lifted. Once replaced, a marked ball is back in play. Understanding these two concepts will make the rest of these examples easy to understand.

If you marked the ball by placing a coin in front of or to the side of the ball (neither is recommended), it must be returned to that very spot. If you fail to do so and play a stroke, you will be guilty of playing from a wrong place. That carries a two-stroke penalty in stroke play and loss of hole in match play (Rule 20-7).

When replacing the ball, it becomes *in play* when it stays *in place* after you replace it—regardless of whether or not you lift your marker. Tiger Woods, among others, likes to replace his ball or have his caddie replace it, but leaves the mark in place. He then lines the putt up, adjusts the brand name or logo for alignment and, only then, lifts his coin. All this is fine, and well within the Rules.

I repeat, the ball is in play when replaced even though you may not have lifted the marker. I've seen golfers replace their ball and *lift* their coin then go to the opposite side of the hole to check their line of putt before returning to rotate or spin their ball in an attempt to align the logo along the line of putt. This would be a penalty because their ball was put back in play when they replaced it and therefore it must be marked (again) if they wanted to lift or even rotate it.

On the flip side, I've seen expert players pick up needless penalties because they misunderstood the Rule, believing their ball was "safe," as long as it their ball was still marked. Here's what I mean. On a very windy day a fellow marked, lifted, cleaned and replaced his ball. However, because of the strong winds he left the marker behind the ball. While lining up the putt the ball began to move and didn't stop until it had rolled completely off the green. The player was certain that he was either required or entitled to replace his ball and did just that. He was wrong.

Decision 20-4/1 is quite explicit on this question. His ball is in play when it is replaced, whether or not the object used to mark its position has been removed. The player received a one-stroke penalty and was required to return the ball to the apron where it had been blown.

I've been asked if there is a penalty for putting without first removing your marker. The answer is no, unless the marker is shaped to provide alignment assistance or you consistently leave the marker behind the ball as some other sort of aid.

Finally, a tip for golfers with bad backs: a ball may be marked and lifted by the player, his partner, or anyone authorized by the player, and must be replaced by the player, his partner or the person who lifted it. So, you don't have to do the bending.

"Plain stupidity," is the way Brian Barnes described his failure to return his ball to the proper position during the final round of the 1998 U.S. Senior Open. His fellow competitor, Jose Maria Canizares, had asked him to move his mark a putter-head to the side—a common request. However, when it came Barnes' turn to putt, he forgot to move the mark back to its original position prior to replacing his ball and he proceeded to putt out. Bad news for Barnes, who then had to add two strokes to his score for the hole, because he had played from a "wrong place."

As maddening as THAT two-stroke penalty can be, the situation can be even worse for players who don't know the rules. Hale Irwin, of all players, received a costly four-stroke penalty lesson when his ball came to rest on a green close to Jim Dent's ball. Both players marked and when it was Irwin's turn to putt, he mistakenly put his ball down at Dent's marker, putted, missed and then realized his mistake. Irwin wanted to do the right thing, which he thought meant accepting the penalty, returning his ball to the proper place and then re-putting. But that was actually his second mistake. Under these circumstances, if a competitor plays a stroke from the wrong place, he must finish the hole and then add two strokes to his score for the hole. Period. He does not "correct" his mistake (unless it was a serious breach) by playing from the proper place. In match play, the penalty is loss of hole.

❦

The Ball. At Rest.

The 1999 U.S. Open at the fabled Pinehurst #2 was memorable as much for the highly polished turtle-back greens and shaved shoulders as for Payne Stewart's fabulous finish. One lasting image was Nick Price sprinting up an embankment onto a green to mark and lift his ball before gravity or Donald Ross' ghost rolled it back to who-knows-where.

The fact that a ball has stopped moving doesn't necessarily mean it will remain "at rest." This is especially true in windy weather on slippery slopes like the putting greens at Pinehurst.

I recall an incident that occurred in a local event a few years ago when a Rules official was called to the 18th green where he found a bewildered competitor deep in conversation with his fellow competitors, caddies and a few spectators.

The player's approach shot had come to rest on the green and about 30 feet *above* the hole. This in itself was improbable, because the green pitches very severely from back to front and was very firm and fast. At any rate, the player had marked his ball, lifted it, then replaced it, all in accordance with the Rules of Golf.

The player then walked to the front of the green to survey the putt from below the hole. As he was looking back up the slope, his ball began to roll down the hill toward him. The ball actually rolled past him and did not stop until it came to rest on the front apron, some 20 feet *below* the hole. The player asked the official for a ruling.

Before the official could provide the answer, two crucial questions had to be answered: 1. Had the ball been in play and at rest after it was replaced, and 2. had the player addressed the ball after he replaced it?

The player's account indicated that the ball had indeed been at rest and in play when it was replaced (Decision 20-3d/1). Further, since the player had not yet addressed the ball before it started rolling, the ball was deemed to be in play where it had come to rest *on the apron*. The player got a good break this time. In fact if the ball had rolled right into the hole he would have been deemed to have holed out on his *previous* stroke. Of course, all luck isn't good and had the ball rolled into the rough, a bunker, a water hazard or even out-of-bounds he would have to live with those results, too.

❧

A Few More Classic Faux Pas...

During the 2003 U.S. Amateur at Oakmont, Matt Johnson's uphill birdie putt ran past the hole. He marked and lifted his ball. However, the ball would not stay put when replaced to its original position, so he moved it to the nearest spot, not nearer the hole, where it would remain at rest. Then, while lining up his putt, the ball rolled down the hill and into the hole! Was it a birdie?

Yes, indeed. Once lifted, the ball was no longer in play but returns to its in play status once it stays at rest *when replaced*. Since Matt had not addressed the ball or caused it to move, he would simply play the ball from wherever it came to rest. Nice birdie Matt!

Davis Love III got an expensive rules lesson during The Players Championship when he accidentally moved his ball with a practice-putting stroke. Since the definition of a *stroke* includes the *intention* of striking the ball Davis' "accident" fell under Rule 18 (Ball at Rest Moved). Since he had caused the ball to move, he should have replaced it and accepted a one-stroke penalty. Instead he thought this "accident" was the same as a *really bad putt* and continued play from that (wrong) place and cost himself another penalty stroke.

I've often been asked what you're supposed to do if the ball just won't stay on the spot it was lifted from when you attempt to replace it. One thing you cannot do is press the ball into the green to make it stay! If it will not remain where replaced you must, without penalty, move the ball to the nearest spot, no closer to the hole, on which it will remain at rest (Rule 20-3d). There may be occasions where you might have to go the apron to find the nearest spot where the ball will remain at rest.

In the Case of an Accident

I once received a call from a confused and disgruntled golfer who believed she had been the unfortunate victim of an incorrect ruling. It seems the caller had accidentally struck her ball while taking a practice swing on a tee, launching it into nearby woods. Unsure how to proceed correctly under the Rules, she asked everyone within earshot for help. After considering the differing opinions, she was convinced she had to play the ball from where it had come to rest.

No one's perfect. Most golfers take great pains to prepare for every shot, but all of us have accidentally moved a ball at one time or another. But, as the telephone call demonstrated, not all us know the correct procedure when such an incident occurs, or that the procedures and penalties can vary depending on where the incident took place.

Our disgruntled friend should have re-teed her ball and proceeded to begin the hole without penalty. That's because, if you accidentally move your ball before putting it into play on a given hole (such as knocking it off the tee), there is no penalty, and the ball must be replaced or re-teed anywhere on the teeing ground. It makes no difference if you moved the ball during a practice swing or otherwise, such as while removing a loose impediment. The key issue is the ball is not in play until you have executed a stroke.

What's the difference between a practice swing and a stroke? By definition, a stroke is "the forward movement of the club made with the intention of fairly striking and moving the ball." A practice swing on the teeing ground that inadvertently moves a ball is therefore not considered a stroke and does not count toward the golfer's score.

However, except in certain circumstances on a putting green, if you accidentally move your ball in any fashion once you have put it into play (including during a practice swing), you incur a penalty of one stroke. You are then required to replace the ball to its original position. If you fail to replace the ball, you are then guilty of playing from a wrong place, which ends up costing you another stroke.

Most golfers are aware that there is a penalty for hitting a ball that is moving (two strokes in stroke play or loss of hole in a match), but few know how the Rules apply if their ball in play moves after they have started their swing and can't stop. Rule 14-5 (Playing Moving Ball) states that when a ball begins to move after the player has begun the stroke, including during the backswing, he shall incur no penalty under this Rule for playing a moving ball. However, if the player had caused the ball to move or had addressed the ball, he would be penalized for moving a ball in play.

My Ball Moved

My ball moved! What do I do? Simple question that deserves a simple reply, right?

Got an answer? Well, if you're like most golfers it would probably be, "replace it—I think! And there's a penalty too—I think?"

If your pal tells you only that his ball, which had been at rest, "moved," the above reply might actually be the most appropriate answer. In fact, if you know where the ball moved from, it must always be replaced unless you "know" it was moved by the wind, water or the like. If you do not know the exact spot it was moved from, it must be dropped as near as possible to its original position. As for a penalty, well, "it depends."

It depends on a number of factors that can only be determined with more information, so a few questions are almost always in order.

Question One: How far did the ball move? By definition, a ball has only "moved" if it leaves its position and comes to rest in another place. So a ball that, lying on the green, oscillates in the wind—or while addressing your ball you touch it so that it rocks forward but comes right back to its original position—has not, under the Rules of Golf, "moved." On the other hand, a ball that sinks just a little deeper into the rough, as you address it perhaps, has moved (Decision 18-1).

Question Two: Who moved it and how was it moved (Rule 18)? If your ball was moved by an outside agency or by a fellow competitor (stroke play), there is no penalty. But you're culpable if you caused the ball to move or if it was moved by your partner or either of your caddies. If it's moved by an opponent, he would suffer a penalty, unless he moved it while helping you search for *your* ball.

Question Three: Where did it happen? Keep in mind that the golf course, all golf courses, are made up of four distinct parts, and the rules can be different for each. Here's an example. If your ball moves as a result of removing loose impediments (Rule 18-2c) on the putting green or the teeing ground of the hole your were playing, there would be no penalty. However, if the ball was anywhere else on the course (*through the green* or in a hazard) you would be penalized.

Question Four: Had you addressed the ball before it moved (Rule 18-2b)? Other than on the teeing ground, if you had, you're in trouble.

The 10-Second Rule

We all like to see the punishment fit the crime. So when young Brian Gay was slapped with a penalty stroke that cost him more than $88,000 for exceeding a time limit by a measly three seconds the public's response was predictable. "What a stupid rule" was one reaction; "another example of an overly regulated game" was another. Here's what happened.

Tied for the lead on the 17th green, during the final round of the 2000 Honda Classic, Gay stood over a 20-foot birdie putt from just off the fringe. If he holed the putt it would put him all alone in the lead with just one hole to play and his best chance for his first PGA Tour victory.

"I hit the putt, and it was right on line," Gay said. "Halfway there, I knew if I—if it got to the hole, it was in. I started walking toward the hole and when I reached I could see the ball was still moving, and (fellow competitor) Jonathan (Kaye) said, 'Wait, it's going to fall.' I kind of peeked up there and looked, it was still (moving), never stopped and then fell in."

As golfers, we've all come face to face with this same scenario and probably have been tempted to do just what Gay did. Convinced that the ball was still moving he waited for it to drop—he waited *13 seconds* for it to drop.

Here's what Rule 16-2 (Ball Overhanging Hole) says: "When any part of the ball overhangs the lip of the hole, the player is allowed enough time to reach the hole without unreasonable delay and an additional 10 seconds to determine whether the ball is at rest. If, by then, the ball has not fallen into the hole, it is *deemed* to be *at rest*. If the ball subsequently falls into the hole, the player is deemed to have holed out with his last stroke, and he shall add a penalty stroke to his score for the hole; otherwise there is no penalty under this rule."

The current Rule was adopted in 1988 so that play would not be unreasonably delayed and so that no one could gain an advantage by waiting more than 10 seconds. The unflappable Don January once waited more than six minutes for his (ball to drop)! In 1985 during the first round of the U.S. Open Denis Watson received the (then) two-stroke penalty for waiting some 30 seconds for his ball to drop. Watson finished only one stroke behind winner Andy North, and the fuss over the ruling led to today's one-stroke penalty.

By the way, no one has suggested that Gay waited the extra time to gain an advantage. He waited because of a common misunderstanding many golfers have when they "know" that their ball "is still moving" and insist that it will "eventually" fall in—although it may take more than 10 seconds. Others may even fear being penalized "for playing a moving ball" if they take a stroke when they "know" the ball is moving.

The Rule, with Decisions to back it up, is very specific on this point. Even if the ball really is moving—if it hasn't fallen into the hole within 10 seconds—it is deemed, or considered, under the rules, to be at rest. And, you will not be permitted to benefit by waiting any longer nor will you be penalized for playing a ball that you "knew," or in fact *was*, actually moving.

In the aftermath of the Brian Gay incident, golfers questioned the meaning of the phrase that says the player is "allowed enough time to reach the hole without unreasonable delay." They also question when the 10-second count actually starts and, finally, want to know who is responsible for timing the ball overhanging the hole, assuming that it was the player's responsibility.

The term "enough time to reach the hole" has been left intentionally non-specific because it would naturally take a player more time to get to his ball after a 50 foot putt than after a 5 footer. The golfer is simply expected to go directly to the hole without undue delay. And it is the golfer himself who is held accountable for the 10-second count. However if, or when, presented with evidence that he has exceeded the 10-second limit *that* evidence would supercede the player's *estimated* time. In this prime-time covered stroke play event with intense TV coverage of the tournament leaders, the whole world could watch, and calculate, the length of time Gay waited for the ball to fall.

Over-regulated game? I don't think so. Tough call? You bet.

But no tougher than telling a player his ball is one inch out of bounds.

Ball in Line of Play

As the 1998 PGA Championship was coming down the stretch, the TV cameras focused on the two players in the day's final group. In fact, as Vijay Singh and Steve Stricker reached the 17th tee, they were the only players with a realistic chance of winning.

Sahalee's 17th hole is a dramatic 200-yard par 3 with a menacing water hazard immediately to the right of the green. Coming off a birdie that brought him to within one stroke of the lead, Stricker hit first and pulled his tee shot into the left bunker. Given a little breathing room, Vijay played away from the water but a bit too safe, and a bad bounce threw his ball in the same bunker and within a foot of his rival's ball. As the players left the teeing ground, the network broke for a commercial. When coverage resumed, Vijay had just played and his ball was rolling toward the hole and we could see Stricker gently placing his ball on the sand.

From a Rules of Golf perspective, the moment the second ball came to rest in the bunker Rule 22 (Ball Interfering with or Assisting Play) was brought front and center with Rule 20-3b (Lie of Ball to be Placed or Replaced Altered) waiting in the wings.

The application of Rule 22 is simple but often misunderstood. In any form of play (match play, stroke play, four-ball, etc.), no matter where your ball comes to rest (putting green, hazard or *through the green*) if a player considers that a ball might interfere with his play (even mentally) he may have that ball lifted. Except on the putting green, the lifted ball may not be cleaned and, to no one's surprise, must be *re*placed—which means put back to the exact spot it was lifted from. This is what happened during the commercial break, and Rule 22 was properly executed.

Now what about Rule 20-3b? What would have happened had Vijay's explosion shot altered Stricker's lie? This was entirely possible given the "peas in a pod" lie of the two balls in the bunker. Clause (iii) under Rule 20-2b tells us that the original lie must be *re-created* as nearly as possible and the ball then placed. In Stricker's case this would have meant a nice clean lie—since that's what he had *before* his lie was altered by Singh's blast. But USGA Decision 20-3b/1 describes a similar situation where two balls came to rest not only in the same bunker, but also in the same heel print! Player A lifted his ball and player B obliterated the heel print while extracting his ball! Player A was then required to re-create the lie he had when he lifted his ball. In other words he had to smooth the area, create a new heel print then place his ball into it.

With few exceptions—and under "equity" (Rule 1-4)—the philosophy the rules follows is that *the player is entitled to the lie and line of play he had when his ball came to rest.* Here are a few examples:

- While you are always permitted to fix *pitch marks* on the putting green if you ELECT to putt from the apron, you may not fix these same pitch marks even if they are on your line of putt on the apron—or anywhere *through the green.* However, take the following circumstance: A player's ball comes to rest in the fairway and just short of a putting green, while another player's shot lands near his ball and creates a pitch-mark so close that it would interfere with the player's lie or line of play. Is the player entitled to relief? Yes. According to Decision 13-2/8, if the pitch-mark was created after the player's ball came to rest he may repair the pitch-mark.

- A's ball is on the apron between the green and a bunker. Another player plays from the bunker and deposits sand on and around A's ball. Is A entitled to relief? Sand is considered a loose impediment only when it lies on a putting green. Therefore, under "normal" conditions it may not be touched *through the green*. However, under "equity" (Rule 1-4) "A" would be entitled to the lie he had when his ball came to rest and, therefore, he would be permitted to lift and clean his ball and remove the sand deposited by the bunker shot without penalty.

- A player's partner, opponent or fellow-competitor plays a stroke from near a bunker and the divot comes to rest near the player's ball lying in the bunker. May the divot be removed? You guessed it. In "equity" the divot may be removed without penalty.

Perhaps the most common manner in which the lie of a ball becomes altered *through the green* is when it is stepped on or driven over leaving the ball embedded in the ground. When this happens, the ball must be placed in the nearest most similar lie, within one club length of its original position and not nearer to the hole. There would be no penalty in stroke play if a fellow competitor or an outside agency moved the ball and altered the lie. However, the player would incur a one-stroke penalty if he, his partner, their equipment or either of their caddies had moved the ball or altered its lie. If your opponent altered the lie of your ball, *he* would incur the penalty unless he was helping you search for your ball.

The Flagstick: A Brief History and Its Place in the Rulebook

Not long ago, the Metropolitan Golf Association conducted a qualifying round for the U.S. Amateur at *my* personal cradle of golf—Willow Ridge Country Club. Cradle of golf? Well, Willow Ridge (formerly Harrison Country Club) was the place where I caddied, learned the game and bought my first set of second-hand clubs—and it brings back wonderful memories every time I visit the property.

On this trip, I recalled an incident that occurred on the fourth hole that almost sent me in search of another line of summer employment—and it had to do with the Rules of Golf.

In golf's formative years the putting green was indistin-
guishable from the fairway. It was 1875 before the flagstick
was even mentioned in the *Rules of Golf*. However, by 1882,
there was a rule requiring the removal of the flagstick whenever your ball was on the putting green. In 1899, a penalty
was assigned to anyone playing a stroke from within 20 yards
of the hole before removing the flagstick. The rule changed a
number of times after the turn of the century, but this rendi-
tion may have been the ancient predecessor to the rule that
led to my own incident.

Golf historians may recall that in the late 1950's there
was no penalty for striking an unattended flagstick from
anywhere, from any distance—even short putts—while the
general penalty applied to a ball that struck an attended or
removed flagstick. This rule may have been very logical, but
the idea of players rapping putts off the flagstick must have
upset the rules makers because by the early 1960's the rule
reverted to a version of the 1899 rule.

Since the rule in effect during some of my caddying days
penalized a player who struck the flagstick with *any shot* from
within 20 yards, I was once directed to attend the flagstick
while an 18-handicapper attempted an explosion shot from a

shallow bunker a mere 25 feet from the hole. Old enough to recognize that I was staring death in the eye, I tried to hide behind the flagstick while simultaneously preparing to "hit the dirt" if my player skulled the shot. Luckily, he shanked it dead right, but I was nonetheless convinced that either this rule would be changed—or my days as a caddie were numbered.

The rule did change again in 1966 and has remained virtually unchanged since. With your ball on the putting green, you will be penalized two strokes in stroke play and loss of hole in a match if your ball strikes the flagstick or an authorized person attending the flagstick. Who's an authorized person? Well, your caddie, partner or your partner's caddie are obviously included, but so is anyone else, such as an opponent, a fellow competitor or even a spectator whom you ask, approve or simply allow to stand near the flagstick before you putt. Bottom line, if you permit someone to attend the flagstick, you'll suffer the consequences if he does not perform his duties correctly.

Commonly, the flagstick is attended only when a player is putting and his ball is on the green. Occasionally, though, you may see someone ask for the flagstick to be attended for a shot from off the green or while playing a blind shot. The player may even ask for someone to stand at the hole and hold the stick high above their head to indicate the location of the hole while he plays. Keep in mind that while this is permitted, the attendee must stand *at the hole* and the player *does* incur a penalty if his ball should strike the stick or the attendee. And remember, never have anyone attend the flagstick while you attempt a short bunker shot—at least not an underage caddie.

Damaged Hole

I remember once watching Tiger Woods loft a towering wedge shot directly into the hole only to have the ball pop back out. It resulted in a tap-in birdie, a badly damaged hole and a Rules question.

Rule 16-1c tells us that a player may repair any damage to the green that was caused by the impact of the ball. Any other damage to the green may *not* be repaired if it might assist the player in his subsequent play of the hole.

Unfortunately, damage to the hole itself is not explicitly covered in the Rules book, so you must go to another source, the *Decisions on the Rules of Golf*, which covers unusual situations not specifically covered by the Rules. The answers to our questions will be there, but it can be tricky.

If the damage to the hole was clearly the result of the impact of a ball (as with Tiger's shot), the player may repair it to the best of his ability. However, if the damage to the hole is not clearly identifiable as a ball mark, "to fix or not to fix" would be the question. And the answer would depend on the extent of the damage.

Let's say a player in a previous group was careless when he removed or replaced the flagstick, or someone stepped too close to the hole. If the damage was such that the proper dimensions of the hole have *not* been substantially changed, the player must continue play without repairing the hole. If he repairs, or even touches the hole under these circumstances, he has violated Rule 16-1a (touching the line of putt) and has incurred a two-stroke penalty or loss of the hole in match play.

If the extent of the damage was more significant, to a degree where the proper dimensions of the hole (4.25 inches in diameter) have been *materially* changed, the player should ask the committee in charge of the competition to have the hole repaired. However, if a committee member is not readily available, the player may repair the damage himself, without penalty. If a player were to repair a materially damaged hole, in competition, when a member of the committee was readily available, he would be penalized under 16-1a.

Under any circumstances, when a hole is badly damaged, the committee should be notified as soon as it is practical so that they can inspect and repair the hole. When it is not possible for a damaged hole to be repaired so that it conforms with the Rules, the committee may make a new hole in a nearby similar position.

Make sense? If it's ball damage, fix it. If not, and the damage is minor, leave it alone until your entire group putts out—then repair it. If the damage materially changes the dimensions of the hole, go ahead and fix it unless you are competing in a tournament and a member of the committee is readily available to assist you.

Golf etiquette also suggests that a courteous player should repair even minor damage to the hole, as well as spike or scuff marks to the green itself, *after holing out*, just as long as he is not doing it to assist any of the players in his group.

You may not hit the hole as often as Tiger Woods, but be prepared to handle a damaged hole should you ever encounter one.

A Word on "Bothersome" Sprinkler Heads

A while back, I was watching a televised PGA Tour event when John Huston "pipelined" his drive down the center of the fairway. Unfortunately, on golf courses, where there are pipe lines there are sprinkler caps, and Huston's ball ended up six inches to the side of one. Huston was not sure whether being this close to the cap entitled him to relief so he called a PGA Tour official over for help.

Since Huston was close to the lead, the TV cameras stayed with him. Viewers got to watch, but could not hear, the animated conversation between Huston and the official, so NBC's Johnny Miller provided verbal subtitles. Miller correctly explained that the sprinkler cap was an immovable obstruction and that Huston would be entitled to relief only if the obstruction interfered with his swing, his stance or the lie of his ball. The question was, did it?

It was obvious to the protagonists, and every viewer, that the cap would not interfere with the lie of his ball nor would it interfere with a normal stance. So, the ongoing discussion must have centered on the question: "Did the obstruction interfere with the area of his intended swing?" Although it was close, it did not look as if Huston's club would hit the sprinkler cap on his swing, since the cap was a full six inches to the side.

At this point, I'm sure many viewers were saying to themselves: "Just how close does the obstruction have to be to the ball to create interference" and qualify a player to get relief? They also might wonder if Huston would get relief for what might be called "mental interference." Miller was obviously thinking along the same lines and commented: "I guess what it comes down to is if the player is *bothered* by the obstruction..." Then Miller cut himself off and never said another word as Huston played his next stroke without incident—and without taking relief.

I cannot tell you the number of times I have been asked to assist a player seeking relief from some condition—casual water, ground under repair, cart path etc.—and my first response is always the same. I politely ask the player to demonstrate that he actually has interference (as defined by the Rules of Golf). In other words, I ask the player to take his stance and simulate a swing so that together we could see if the obstruction actually did interfere with his stance or would interfere with his swing.

Miller had accurately and concisely defined what would constitute interference and when it got right down to it, the official concluded that the cap did not interfere with his swing. Huston might have been "bothered" by the cap, but that would have been irrelevant. He did not qualify for relief, because the obstruction (in this case the sprinkler cap) did not have interfere with (been struck by) his club during a normal swing. Nor had the obstruction interfered with his stance or the lie of the ball.

Similarly, and despite the common misconception, there is no relief *through the green* if an immovable obstruction simply lay between you and the hole (i.e., your ball came to rest 10 feet behind a water fountain), even if the obstruction did intervene on the line of play. Where immovable obstructions are concerned, you are not entitled to relief unless there is "real" interference" *as defined by the Rules of Golf.*

By the way, if the cap had been the same six inches in front of his ball, Huston very well might have been entitled to relief because a normal follow-through more than likely would have struck the cap. This helps to point out that proximity of a ball to an obstruction is not the only factor—and just one of many—that needs to be considered to determine if interference exists and if relief is justified.

Obstructions: To Move or Not to Move?

An *obstruction* is anything artificial whether erected, placed or left on the course. Artificially surfaced cart paths, irrigation heads, control boxes and rain shelters are examples of *immovable* obstructions. Obstructions that can be moved without unreasonable effort or delay or without doing damage to the course (i.e., bunker rakes, paper cups and soda cans) are considered *movable* obstructions.

The relief procedures for movable and immovable obstructions are quite different. To take relief from a movable obstruction, you simply move the obstruction! To gain relief from interference with an immovable obstruction, you must drop the ball within a club length of the nearest point of relief. Therefore, it is important to know the difference and to realize that the committee in charge may decree a movable obstruction to be immovable!

A recent British Open was a case in point. During Friday's second round at Carnoustie, Tiger Woods was *directed* by a referee to treat a bundle of TV cables as an immovable obstruction and the *required* relief may have led to an improved situation for Tiger—and a controversy among interested golfers, spectators and the media. Why did the referee decide that the cables (which looked like a movable obstruction) should be treated as immovable? Well, the Rules say that an obstruction is a *movable* obstruction if it may be moved (1) without unreasonable effort; (2) without unduly delaying play; and (3) without causing damage. Otherwise, it is deemed to be immovable.

After inspecting the bundle of cables the referee came to the decision that they could not be moved without unreasonable effort and therefore they must be treated as immovable—after the fact, there was a question as to whether he was correct.

A more common, and recommended, use of this type of committee discretion deals with stakes and cables used to support newly planted trees. If it was to his advantage a healthy, perhaps burly, golfer might be able to remove a stake so that he could play from a favorable lie rather than moving the ball as required to find relief if the stake and cable were not designated as immovable. Why the recommendation? Well, the stakes and cable are on the course for a very specific purpose: to support a tree that needs support. If players were allowed to remove these stakes, it would no longer provide support for the tree. Many golf associations routinely declare these types of stakes and cables to be immovable and recommend this procedure to member clubs.

Using this line of logic and under "preservation of the course" the committee can also require a player to take relief when his ball comes to rest in certain sensitive areas such as decorative flower beds, turf nurseries or newly sodded or seeded areas. When advisable, the committee should mark or declare these areas as "Ground Under Repair" and announce that relief is mandatory.

Another instance where a committee might use its authority to change the status of what might otherwise be an obstruction deals with "integral parts of the course." An example might be the windmill at The National Golf Links of America in Southampton, NY. An international icon would be the greenside road on St Andrews' famous 17th—the "Road Hole." When so designated, these artificial objects do not provide the "free relief" their more common relatives do.

What to Do about Loose Impediments

New golfers may not know for sure what loose impediments are, but knowing what they are and what you are entitled to do with them could save you an occasional stroke.

Loose impediments are *natural* objects such as fallen branches, stones, leaves, and twigs that are not fixed or growing, are not solidly embedded in the ground and are not adhering to the ball. A pine cone that has fallen from a tree, for example, is a loose impediment, in that it's a natural object, and no longer fixed or growing. Bunker rakes, cigarette butts and soda cans are not loose impediments in that although they may not be fixed and probably are not growing, they are man-made and considered *movable obstructions*.

In most instances, a golfer can move loose impediments. But this is not always the case, and there can be certain "provisos" attached.

To help you follow correct procedure, think of the golf course as four areas: (1) teeing ground; (2) putting greens; (3) hazards and (4) *through the green*—which covers the rest of the course.

The teeing ground. Before you put a ball into play, you may remove any loose impediments. If your ball moves, you may replace it or move to another part of the teeing ground without penalty.

The putting green. The Rule is similar here, except that if your ball moves as you remove the loose impediment, it must be replaced—again, without penalty. Keep in mind that sand and loose soil are considered loose impediments only on the putting green. Since the apron is not part of the putting green, you are not permitted to brush away sand on your line of play on the apron even if it interferes with your stroke.

Hazards. When your ball is in a hazard, you may not move or even touch loose impediments that also lie in the hazard. If you do touch them, even on your backswing, you lose the hole in a match and incur a two-stroke penalty in stroke play.

Through the green. You may remove all loose impediments. However, if the removal of a loose impediment causes your ball to move, you incur a penalty stroke and must replace your ball. So, be very careful when your ball comes to rest in a precarious lie littered with leaves, sticks or pine needles!

I've been asked what you can do if your stance or swing is interfered with by a large detached branch which is impossible to move, even with assistance, without disrupting and moving your ball. Under these circumstances, it is good to know that you may break off part of the branch—without penalty.

Finally, a word of advice. When required to drop a ball *through the green*, you may clear the area of any loose impediments before dropping. A "rules wise" golfer knows that if there are any loose impediments in the area, it is better to remove them *before* you drop than risk penalty by removing them after you drop.

❦

Twigs, Pebbles and...Tiger's Boulder

Here's a Rules situation that created a lot of discussion. Tiger Woods, hot on the heels and playing with eventual Phoenix Open winner Rocco Mediate, had just pulled his tee ball into the desert. No problem. Except for the small boulder which was right in front of Tiger's ball. What to do? Well he could pitch the ball back to the fairway, he could declare it unplayable and drop away from the boulder or—wait a minute—he could enlist a dozen or so members of his gallery to help roll the boulder out of the way.

After checking the "legality" of option three with a member of the PG Tour Rules staff, Tiger put out the call for a few stout-hearted men and, by putting the shoulder to the boulder, they paved the way for a Woods birdie. The scene was reminiscent of one of those Scottish Highlands games—you know, tossing a log or pulling a locomotive—and they probably set the Guinness Record for the largest loose impediment ever moved.

I've often been asked how big something has to be before it loses its status as a loose impediment. My answer is "if you, and anyone available and willing to help you, can move it without delaying play it doesn't matter how big it is." So, despite the comments by a dubious and incredulous Ken Venturi (and the second-guessing of many), the assistance Tiger received was absolutely by the book—the *Decision on the Rules of Golf* book, of course.

Decision 23-1/2 clarifies the status of a very large stone as a loose impediment by stating that, "stones of any size (as long as they are not solidly embedded in the ground) are loose impediments and may be removed, provided removal does not unduly delay play." And Decision 23-1/3 gives the "OK" for a player to enlist spectators, caddies, fellow-competitors, etc., to assist in the removal of extra large samples.

While thumbing through the *Decisions* that related to Tiger's situation, I found a few more points that might be of interest. When is a stone solidly embedded? The USGA's answer: "If a stone is partially embedded and may be picked up with ease, it is a loose impediment. However, if there is any doubt as to whether a stone is solidly embedded or not, it should not be removed." Here's another. Is an embedded acorn a loose impediment? Answer: Sure it is, but not if it is solidly embedded. Have you ever had an acorn embedded on your line of putt? If you have, and resorted to digging the acorn out of the green with a wooden tee or green repair tool, it was not a loose impediment and you were in violation of Rule 16-1. The acorn, like a stone, is only a loose impediment if it can be easily removed—not dug out!

I'm sure you've seen this happen. A player hits his ball onto a gravel-covered road. Even though he is entitled to relief from this obstruction, he prefers to play the ball from the road. May he remove gravel that might interfere with his stroke? You bet he can. Gravel is a loose impediment and the player's right to remove it is not canceled by the fact that, when a road is covered with gravel, it becomes an artificially surfaced road and thus an obstruction.

The Meanings of Stakes

Wooden and plastic stakes are common enough around a golf course and, depending on their purpose and color, have several different rules applications.

Stakes are often used to define the margins of water hazards. Yellow stakes denote regular water hazards and red stakes lateral water hazards.

If a *hazard* stake is readily moveable, it would be classified as a moveable obstruction. To gain relief, you would simply move the stake.

However, if a stake is solidly embedded into the ground and could not be moved without unreasonable effort, without unduly delaying play or causing damage, it would be classified as an immovable obstruction. *As* with any other immovable obstruction, you would gain relief by finding the nearest point of relief then dropping your ball within a club length of that point, but not nearer to the hole.

If your ball lies outside, but near, a water or lateral hazard and a yellow or red hazard stake interfered with your stance, the lie of your ball or the area of your intended swing you would be entitled to relief. However, if your ball lies *in* a water or lateral water hazard the situation changes.

A note under Rule 24 says "if a ball lies in or touches a water hazard, or lateral water hazard, the player is not entitled to relief without penalty from interfering *immovable* obstructions."

Always keep in mind that an obstruction is classified as moveable or immovable based on its ease of movement. If it can be easily moved, it is a movable obstruction. So, even if your ball lies *in* a water hazard, if an interfering hazard stake is easily moved, you *may* remove the stake. However, if the stake would be defined as an immovable obstruction—and your ball is in the hazard- you would *not* be entitled to any relief without penalty.

White stakes are commonly used to define the boundaries of the course itself and are considered "fixed" parts of the course and, therefore, they *are not obstructions*. If you have interference with an out-of-bounds stake, you are not permitted to remove the stake under any circumstances, even if it happens to be readily moveable. If you were to remove or even move an out-of-bounds stake, you would incur a two-stroke penalty or loss of hole in a match.

Stakes are also used, alone or with a cable, to support new plantings or weakened trees and occasionally give rise to rules controversies. Unless a local rule is in effect, relief is available for interference by the stake and cable only—not for interference by the tree itself. And, it is good to know that the club committee or course staff may, and should, deem the stakes to be immovable obstructions, which would mean that if you take relief it must be by moving the ball, not the stake.

When Cartpaths Get in the Way

Every weekend, whether it's in a friendly four-ball or the PGA Tour, someone looks for relief from an artificially surfaced cartpath. And too often, the rule involved is misapplied. Here's a quick look at how, when and where to take such relief.

Determine if you have interference. Sounds pretty elementary, but keep in mind that interference occurs only when your ball lies on the cartpath or so close to it that the path interferes with your stance or the area of your intended swing. This means interference with your line of play or "mental interference," do not constitute interference.

You can claim interference, however, if your ball lies off the cartpath and a normal takeaway or follow-through would strike the path, or if you have to stand on the path in order to play your next stroke.

To determine whether you have interference, you must take a normal stance and address your ball with the club that you would expect to use for your next stroke. However, if it's necessary and reasonable to play the next stroke with an unusual stance (and that stance causes interference), you are entitled to relief but you may not take an unusual stance, or use a longer club than necessary, just to create interference.

Determine the nearest point of relief. If you have interference and your ball lies *through the green*, you must determine the point nearest to the ball that (a) is not nearer to the hole; (b) avoids all interference; and (c) is not in a hazard or on a putting green. Please note that nothing was said about going to the nearest side of the cartpath.

That's not always the nearest point of relief. The recommended procedure for determining the nearest point of relief is: (1) to address your ball with the club you would expect to use for the next stroke; (2) then move to the closest point (fulfilling the requirements spelled out in a, b and c, above) where your swing and stance are free from the interference; and (3) stand at this point and place a tee in the ground on the spot where your ball would be. This spot is the nearest point of relief.

If the original position of the ball is such that it is not perfectly clear which direction will yield the nearest point of relief, use the above procedure to determine two or more *possible* nearest points. Then, simply measure the distance from where the ball lies to each possible point. The point that is the shortest distance from where your ball lies is the nearest point of relief and must be used. You can't choose one point over another (or one side of the cartpath over the other) simply because it will give you a more favorable shot.

To sum up... Measure one club-length from the nearest point of relief — *then* decide if relief is the best option. Using *any club in your bag*, measure a distance of one club length from the nearest point of relief. If you decide to take relief you must drop your ball within this club-length.

You may have noted that, up to this point, we haven't mentioned marking, lifting or even touching your ball. This is because a smart player examines the area in which he would be required to drop the ball *before* he elects to take relief, and then determines if he's better off taking the free relief or playing the ball from where it lies. There are occasions when it might be wiser to punch a shot off the cartpath than to try to hack the ball out of tall rough or out from behind a tree. Remember that although Rule 24 provides relief from the obstruction, it doesn't guarantee a clear shot—or any shot at all, for that matter.

If you do decide that taking relief from the cartpath is the best option, you should now lift your ball and clean it, if necessary. You're not required to mark the ball's position before you lift it, but it's always a good idea. *Now drop the ball into the required area.*

Relief: Choosing the Nearest Point

One of my favorite players was Dave Stockton. The two-time

PGA winner's swing may never be likened to Byron Nelson's, but his course management and competitive nature made him a player to watch whenever he was in contention.

I remember watching him cling to a two-stroke lead in a head-to-head battle with Bob Murphy, during the 1996 U.S. Senior Open when his long approach overshot the putting surface and came to rest on the back apron in an area marked as ground under repair.

The *nearest point of relief* for ground under repair is defined as the "nearest point on the course which avoids interference by the condition, is not nearer to the hole, in a hazard or on a putting green." Since Stockton clearly had interference by the ground under repair, he was *entitled* to relief without penalty and would be *permitted* to lift and clean his ball and drop it within a club length of his nearest point of relief. However, before lifting his ball (which would have signaled his intention to take relief), Stockton surveyed the area and realized that his nearest point of relief was behind the green on a very steep slope, and in heavy rough to boot! Stockton wanted no part of a tricky downhill pitch, so he opted to pass up the free relief and play the ball from where it had come to rest—in the ground-under-repair area—and made the ensuing "up and down" look professionally routine.

His decision highlights two points involving relief procedures that are often overlooked and misunderstood. First, once you pick up your ball, whether you mark its position or not, you will not be allowed to return the ball to its original position without penalty. And, second, relief from conditions, such as ground under repair or an artificially surfaced cartpath, does not guarantee you a good lie or even a fair opportunity to play your next stroke, nor is it supposed to. It only assures that you will get out of the ground under repair, or off the cart path, without penalty.

This is why Stockton gave a critical eye to the area where he would be required to drop *before* he picked up his ball. Inexperienced players often make the mistake of picking up their ball the moment they realize that they are *entitled* to take relief, *then* figure out where their nearest point of relief is! Keep in mind that there is only one nearest point of relief, and if that point (and one club length) turns out to be behind a large tree, in deep rough or even in a bush, a player who has already lifted his ball would either have to live with those circumstances or accept a penalty stroke to return his ball to its original position.

Another example is Todd Hamilton in the 2004 British Open. Hamilton was clinging to a one-stroke lead and in a heated battle with super-star Ernie Els when he pulled his approach to the final green into deep British Open rough. He had to be pleased to find his ball in a playable lie but disappointed that his backswing was restricted by a spectator barrier. While the barrier might have looked movable, it had been designated by the Championship Committee as an immovable obstruction. So, if Hamilton wanted relief from the fence, he would have to move the ball.

The conundrum: Hamilton had interference and was entitled to relief but had a remarkably good lie versus taking relief, dropping in the heavy rough, risking an awful lie and almost guaranteeing an impossible up-and-down.

The nearest point of relief for immovable obstructions (Rule 24) is defined as the "nearest point on the course which avoids interference by the condition, is not nearer to the hole, in a hazard or on a putting green." Since Hamilton clearly had interference, he was entitled to relief without penalty and would be permitted to lift and clean his ball and drop it within a club length of his "nearest point of relief." However, before lifting his ball (which would have signaled his intention to take relief), Hamilton smartly surveyed the area and realized that his nearest point of relief was in thick, gnarly rough, so he thought long and hard before finally deciding to take his chances, despite the restricted backswing, in favor of a playable lie.

So, take a lesson from Dave Stockton and Todd Hamilton: Don't pick it up until you've checked out where you're going to be required to drop it!

One Bad Drop Deserves Another

How often have we seen a PGA Tour star take a drop only to see him pick it up and drop it again? Rule 20-2 deals with dropping and re-dropping and reminds us that a ball to be dropped must be dropped by the player himself—no designated droppers allowed! The Rule goes on to say that the player must stand erect and hold the ball at shoulder height and arm's length when he drops it. If a ball is dropped by anyone other than the player himself, or in any other manner, and is not picked up and dropped properly, the player incurs a penalty stroke.

If the ball touches the player or his equipment before or after it hits a part of the course, it must be re-dropped, without penalty, and there is no limit to the number of times you get to drop it until you drop it properly! However, if the ball is dropped correctly and in the correct place, there are seven (and only seven) circumstances that would require a player to re-drop: (1) If your dropped ball rolled into a hazard (bunker or water hazard) or (2) rolled out of a hazard you must re-drop (keep in mind that there are times when you might choose, or be required, to drop in a hazard such as relief from casual water in a bunker). You must also re-drop if (3) your dropped ball rolls out of bounds or (4) rolls onto a putting green. By the way this is very different from a dropped ball rolling onto the fairway after dropping in the rough or vice versa, which, by itself, would not require, or allow, a re-drop.

The occurrence of one of these first four "required re-drop" situations may seem a bit remote but the final three scenarios occur all the time and are often misunderstood and mishandled. You must re-drop your ball if (5) you take relief from an immovable obstruction or abnormal ground conditions (ground under repair, casual water, etc.) and your dropped ball rolls into a position where you still have interference from the condition you took relief from; (6) your dropped ball comes to rest more than two club lengths from where it first struck a part of the course; or (7) your dropped ball rolls and comes to rest nearer to the hole than its original position, nearest point of relief or the point your ball last crossed the margin of a water hazard.

When re-dropped, if the ball should again roll and come to rest in any of these seven positions, you must lift the ball and place it as near as possible to the spot where it first struck a part of the course on the second drop.

By the way, just to resolve any doubt: You are required to go through the formality of dropping the ball twice before placing it, even if it is obvious that the ball will probably roll right into a position requiring a re-drop. If you did place it when you were supposed to drop (or re-drop) or dropped it a third time instead of placing it, you could correct your mistake without penalty. However, if you fail to correct one of these errors, and play your next stroke, you would incur a two-stroke penalty in stroke play or loss of hole in a match.

We've all seen occasions where drop areas or drop circles have been designated. When you opt to drop in such an area, keep in mind that the ball needs only to be dropped in that area—it need not come to rest in the drop area—and a re-drop would be required only if the ball comes to rest in one of the "big seven" noted above.

Please take note: "I didn't like the lie I got on the first drop!" was never mentioned as a reason to re-drop, despite its popularity.

In the Drink: Taking Lateral Hazards Literally

Hall of Fame baseball umpire Bill Klem enjoyed reminding catchers of his authority when they inquired as to the status of a borderline pitch: "It ain't nothin' 'till I call it (a ball or a strike)!" Similarly, a body of water is neither a water hazard nor a lateral water hazard until the club's committee has carried out its responsibility to determine the status of all of the ponds, lakes, streams and rivers on the course (whether dry or not) and marked their boundaries or *margins*.

Despite the common misconception, a body of water is not automatically a *lateral water hazard* just because it happens to parallel a fairway. In fact, all hazards should be played as water hazards (yellow stakes or lines), unless it is impossible or impractical to require the player, when taking relief, to drop while keeping the point his ball last crossed the margin of the hazard between him and the hole.

What makes it impossible or impractical? The Pacific Ocean on Pebble Beach's 18th hole is a "lateral" (red stakes or lines) because it would be impossible to keep most points a ball would last cross the margin of *that* hazard between the place you drop and the hole—without going to Japan, that is!

It might be similarly impractical to mark as a water hazard a narrow stream that runs down the right side of the fairway with heavy underbrush to *its* right, because that might force players to take a penalty *then* drop in the underbrush by requiring them to keep the point the ball last crossed the margin between them and the hole.

While a player may always choose to play his ball from within a hazard, if he opts to take relief from a *water* hazard his only options are (1) stroke and distance or (2) drop keeping the point his ball last crossed the margin of the hazard between him and the hole. When the hazard has been marked as a "lateral water hazard," the player has two *additional* options. He may (3) drop a ball outside the hazard, within two club lengths of the point it last crossed the margin of the lateral hazard, but not nearer to the hole or (4) go to the *opposite margin* of the hazard, to a point *equal* distance from the hole, and drop a ball within two club lengths of that point.

Disputes over where to drop when there is *knowledge or virtual certainty* that a ball ended up in a water hazard are common and generally created on two fronts. The first is a misunderstanding of the real difference between the two types of water hazards and the second is a misuse of the phrase "point of entry."

It may be a mouthful, but Rule 26 refers to "the point where a ball last crosses the margin of the hazard"—not the "point of entry," a phrase the Rules of Golf never uses because it is just not specific enough.

For one thing, *point of entry* means entering the water to some people, which may be irrelevant. What is relevant is where the ball enters the hazard, keeping in mind that the margin of the hazard and the actual water line are seldom the same.

Have you ever hit a ball into a water hazard only to watch it skip off the water, exit the hazard, hit a tree *or rock on the other side* and re-enter the hazard? The ball actually had two "points of entry" into the hazard! If *your* reference point to drop is the "point of entry" where your ball *first* entered the hazard, mine is the "point the ball *last* crossed the margin," we might be talking about two different places and headed for one of those "disputes" I referred to earlier.

When a ball comes to rest in a water hazard, the player has three options: he may (1) attempt to play the ball where it lay; he may (2) take a one-stroke penalty and replay the stroke (stroke and distance); or (3) drop a ball behind the hazard keeping the point it *last* crossed the margin of the hazard directly between the hole and the spot on which the ball is dropped with no limit to how far behind the hazard the ball may be dropped.

The Strict Rules of Casual Water

In many parts of the U.S., the end of winter and early spring golf are sure to be affected by two conditions: casual water and *embedded balls*. But heavy rains or over-watering can create the same situations.

Casual water is any temporary accumulation of water that is visible before or after the player takes his stance and which is not in a water hazard. The key word here is "visible," because casual water is not mud or soft ground, and you are not entitled to relief if you merely "hear" or "feel" water under your feet.

Through the green you obtain relief from casual water by dropping the ball, not nearer to the hole, within a club length of the nearest point of relief. In a bunker you gain relief by dropping the ball, in the bunker, as near as possible to the spot where it lay, but not nearer the hole on a spot where you have gained "maximum" relief. Please note that you do not place the ball in the bunker, even though dropping may result in a "fried-egg" lie.

There are three questions that are often asked about "plugged" or embedded balls. Exactly what constitutes an embedded ball? Where do I drop when taking relief? Am I permitted to clean my ball before I drop it?

"An embedded ball is a ball which is embedded in its own pitch mark in the ground in any closely mown area through the green." This definition, when read carefully, is intended to deny relief to a ball that merely rolled into a real bad lie or even into someone else's pitch mark because it limits relief to a ball in its "own" pitch mark.

The definition is also intended to deny relief to a ball buried or cupped in deep or matted grass unless it had actually embedded into the soil.

If there is any question as to whether your ball is embedded, you are permitted to mark its position and lift it to check. If it didn't qualify as an embedded ball you must put it back where you lifted it from and either play it from the bad lie or declare it unplayable and take a one-stroke penalty.

The phrase *closely mown area* would also reject relief to a player whose ball embedded in the rough. If this seems unfair or contradicts your understanding of embedded balls, take heart. The USGA, professional Tours and virtually all American golf associations conduct every event using a local rule, which expands relief for embedded balls from closely mown areas to anywhere *through the green*—regardless of the height of the grass. Establishing this local rule is the responsibility of the committee in charge of your course or event.

So, if your course has announced, and put the "Local Embedded Ball Rule" into effect (as it should), you are entitled to relief if your ball happens to embed itself: (1) in the ground; (2) in its own pitch mark; or (3) outside of a bunker or hazard.

The answers to our other two questions are simple, at least by comparison. When permitted to take relief for an embedded ball, the ball must be dropped as near as possible to where it had been embedded, but not nearer to the hole. You do not get to drop two or even one club length away. "As near as possible" means a few inches, and you cannot fix "the pitch mark" until after you play your stroke.

And finally, yes, you may clean your ball before you drop it, just as you may clean it if you opt to take relief from casual water or from an obstruction or ground under repair.

Bunker or Trap, Know the Rules

For some, it can be like Br'er Rabbit's Laughin' Place, for others Dante's Inferno. It can make the difference between an exhilarating "save" and a devastating double-bogey.

The subject is sand traps or, more properly, bunkers. While you may deal with water hazards occasionally and unplayable lies infrequently, you face a potential battle with the sand on virtually every hole.

When any part of the ball touches a bunker, the ball is considered "in" the bunker and the player would not be permitted to ground his club, test the surface, build a stance or touch loose impediments like leaves, sticks or stones that lie within that bunker. It is important here to remember the difference between loose impediments and small movable obstructions like cigarette butts, loose paper or plastic cups, which may always be moved without penalty.

Nearly every golfer has experienced the frustration of a ball that buried into the sand in a virtually unplayable position. Before attempting the impossible, remember that you have the option of declaring the ball "unplayable" and, with a one-stroke penalty, moving it under three different options. You may drop the ball within two club lengths of the spot it had buried (no nearer to the hole) or keep that spot between you and the hole and go back as far as you like. With both of these options, the ball must be dropped in the bunker. However, often overlooked is the option to get out of the bunker by returning to the place where you hit the last shot from to drop.

Worse than a buried lie is the ball that completely disappears into soft sand. The ball would have to be considered lost if you could not find it within five minutes, but you should remember that you, and those willing to help, can probe for the ball with a club or even a rake in an effort to find the ball. If you do find the ball, you must re-create the buried lie and are permitted to remove just enough sand to see where the ball is.

One rule that many golfers find unfair deals with casual water in a bunker. If casual water interferes with your stance or lie you are permitted to take the maximum available relief. However, you must not go nearer to the hole to gain relief and you must drop the ball within the bunker, which often results in a difficult fried-egg lie. Worse yet, if the maximum available relief provided little or no practical relief, the golfer would be forced to play the ball where it lay, declare it unplayable or drop it behind the bunker with a one-stroke penalty.

Using the Unplayable Ball Rule with Cleverness

While no one ever cheerfully elects to accept a penalty stroke, declaring your ball unplayable may be the most rational decision you can make to extricate yourself from a truly impossible situation. Considering how infrequently the PGA Tour stars actually get into really serious trouble, I think you'd find that they actually use Rule 28 (Ball Unplayable) more than we common folk. One reason may be that they are almost always competing at stroke play, where one disastrous hole could cost them thousands of dollars. But more likely it's because they have learned that the odds of pulling off a one-in-a-million shot are accurate. There is something for all of us to learn from their restraint and patience.

While Tiger Woods' victory at St Andrews certainly stamped 2005 as "year of the Tiger," who's to say that Tiger would have won were it not for the benefits of the "Unplay-able Ball" rule (Rule 28)? "Benefits," you say? You bet!

In golf's earliest days there was no such thing as relief from an unplayable lie. Golf's pioneers would simply hack their way out of near-impossible situations and watch their scores soar. Of course golf was an almost exclusively match play game in those days so a battle with the gorse that resulted in a quadruple bogey only meant you were one down—not four strokes behind.

As the game grew and stroke play became a more common game, the unplayable ball Rule was added so that one errant shot would no longer turn the leader into an also-ran. Keep in mind that Woods went bogey-par during his two third-round unplayable situations in the gorse. And, he went on for an ultimate four-stroke victory. So, in a way, he did "benefit" by the existence and intelligent use of Rule 28.

Having made the decision to declare your ball unplayable, you have a second decision to make: Which relief option to select? The Rules offer three courses of action, and each includes a one-stroke penalty. You may: (a) play a ball from as near as possible to the spot you played your previous stroke (stroke and distance); (b) drop and play within two club-lengths of the spot where the ball lay, but not nearer to the hole; or (c) drop and play behind the point where the ball lay, keeping that point directly between the hole and the spot on which the ball is dropped, with no limit on how far behind that point the ball may be dropped.

Retracing your steps and accepting a stroke-and-distance penalty always feels like the most onerous of penalties, which is probably why it is usually our last choice—or never even considered. Picture this: you drive your ball deep into an area of high fescue grass into a truly unplayable lie. Option "c" only takes you further into the deep grass and option "b" only moves you two club lengths *closer* to a playable lie. All the options are available but only option "a" is practical. This is often the case.

Please note that the phrase "nearest point of relief" does not apply when you've declared your ball unplayable—but it is often *mis*applied. Here is an example: After your perfect drive, your opponent's tee shot comes to rest snug against the trunk of a towering Douglas fir whose lowest boughs are close to the ground and reach out 20 feet in every direction. You crawl in, identify the ball as yours, and actually consider an impossible punch-out—from your knees! When you realize that you cannot even take a backswing, you declare it unplayable. You could go back far enough to get this ball around or over the tree, but this would mean giving up a lot of distance and no guarantee of a clear shot. Too often players faced with this predicament will *improperly* drop to the side of the tree at the nearest point of relief. Remember, the two club-lengths must be measured from where the ball lay which, in this case, would not get you out from under the tree.

Most golfers are reluctant to use the Unplayable Ball Rule—and accept the one-stroke penalty that accompanies each of the relief options—not wishing to "give up" a stroke but going for the one-in-a-million miracle shot instead. They usually find that the odds were pretty accurate.

Hey, if it's good enough for Tiger, it may be worth considering for ourselves.

A Few Common Misconceptions Concerning the Ball

Golf is one of the few sports, even at the highest levels, where each player provides his own ball. However, despite the fact that we may go through a gross a year there are still certain misunderstandings regarding golf balls.

- Just what constitutes a "legal" ball?
- When am I permitted to change or clean my golf ball?
- What is the difference between a provisional ball and a second ball?
- Why is it that I can't find the one-ball rule in the Rules book?
- What is the "correct" way to mark and lift your ball?

When golfers agree to play "USGA Rules" they have agreed to play only balls that conform to USGA's specifications regarding weight and size and other technical requirements. Competitors on the PGA Tour or in most events conducted by a recognized golf association may be limited to the use of balls listed on the USGA *Conforming Ball List*, which includes virtually all the popular brands and is regularly updated.

If you asked 10 people what the one-ball rule is you'd probably get 10 different answers. And you will not find it under the *Rules of Play* in the Rules book. For one thing, it is not a Rule of Golf but rather a local rule that is used only at the discretion of the committee in charge of the competition.

The one-ball rule, when used, limits a player to the use of the same brand and type ball for the entire round. He is not limited to the use of just one ball for the whole round or even for a whole hole. He could swap a Titleist 2 for a Titleist 3, but if he starts out with a Titleist Pro V1 he could not switch to a Titleist Pro V1x: He must stay with the exact same type of ball for the entire round.

Whether the one-ball rule is in effect or not, you can always change balls between play of holes or substitute another ball if you lose your original, hit it OB, declare it unplayable, or hit it into a water hazard.

You may also substitute a new ball for one that has become *unfit for play* during the hole being played. Of course, this means you can't start out on a water hole with a cut-up old clunker with plans to change to a new putting ball once you reach the green.

By the way, a ball is considered unfit for play (Rule 5-3) only if it is visibly cut, cracked or out of shape.

If you have reason to believe your ball has become unfit, you may lift it without penalty to determine if, in fact, it is unfit. Before lifting the ball, you must tell your opponent, your marker or one of your fellow competitors and you must give them the opportunity to examine the ball and to observe the lifting and replacing of the ball. You are required to mark the ball's position before you lift it and you are not permitted to clean it.

Everyone knows that you are permitted to clean your ball after lifting it from the putting green (Rule 16-1b). But many golfers forget that they are allowed to clean their ball virtually every time they are permitted to lift it (ground under repair, embedded ball, casual water etc.). In fact, the only times you are *not* permitted to clean it after lifting it is when you lift it to determine if it is unfit for play, because it is interfering or assisting play of another ball or when you lift it for identification (Rule 21).

A provisional ball (Rule 27-2) is a *time-saving courtesy* extended to a player whose ball may be out of bounds or lost outside a water hazard.

Without the use of a provisional, if the original ball is lost, a player's only option would be to waste time walking all the way back to the spot he just played from. A "second ball" may be *used only in stroke play* when a player is in doubt about the rules or the procedures he is supposed to follow. If you find yourself in a tricky situation you should announce your decision to invoke this Rule (3-3) *before* taking any further action (like taking relief or playing another stroke). You must also announce which of the two balls you want to have counted if the ruling goes your way. You must then play out the hole with both balls and report all the facts to the committee before turning in your scorecard.

PART THREE

Partners, Caddies & Equipment

Partners in Punishment

For many of us, team competition can often be more intense than individual play, perhaps because when we play in a team format we are at the same time comforted and burdened by the very existence of a partner. One way to avoid problems when playing with a partner is to understand the rules that apply to team competition. As you establish your game plan for your next team tournament or match, try to keep the following things in mind:

- Technically, partners can share clubs—as long as the total number of clubs carried by the two players doesn't exceed 14. For example, if you decide to share clubs with your partner but still want to use your own driver and putter, the two of you would be limited to a *total* of only 12 other clubs. Since most people usually carry a full set of clubs, this rule is rarely applicable or helpful, because if you're both playing with your own clubs you cannot borrow one of your partners clubs—even if you lose or break a valuable club such as a putter or sand wedge.

- Your partner may, of course, help you search for a lost ball. But remember, if he moves the ball, even accidentally, during the search, or if he improves the area of your intended swing by pressing down grass or breaking branches, it is *you* who suffers the penalty!

- Partners may play in the order that the side considers best. This means that it's okay to have your partner tap in a short putt for par when it's your turn to play so that you can have a "free run" with your 40-foot birdie attempt (Rule 30-3c). However, if your opponents "concede" your partner's bogey putt, which happens to be on the same line as your birdie try, *you* will be out of the hole if your partner insists on putting the ball, anyway, so that you can "go to school" on his putt.

- Your team will be penalized if you, or your partner, begin the round with more than 14 clubs. This can really hurt: Let's say you start the round with birdies on the first two holes to send your team two-up! Your partner starts bogey/double bogey, then discovers that he has an extra club in his bag. The penalty (loss of hole) is applied to the "state of the match," which means your team just dropped back to all square!

- Worse than having too many clubs would be a situation where your partner carried a non-conforming club, played a club whose playing characteristics had been altered (other than in the normal course of play) or played a non-conforming ball. If this happens, you are both *disqualified*!

- Finally, if your partner breaches a rule and it assists you or adversely affects your opponents, *you* incur the applicable penalty (Rule 30-3f). For example, say that you lie two in a bunker. Within a foot of your ball, but lying four, is your partner's ball, and interfering with both balls is a small branch. If your partner removes the branch, he is penalized for violating Rule 13-4, and you are penalized because his rule violation assisted you!

What's the best way to avoid these pitfalls of partnerships? You can go it alone, but it might be better to give your favorite partner a copy of the Rules of Golf—and maybe a weekly quiz.

The Caddie

One of golf's grandest traditions is the caddie. Caddies were there for Old Tom Morris, Francis Ouimet and Tiger Woods, and hopefully they'll remain a part of the fabric of the game forever.

A caddie can be a trusted advisor, an empathetic psychologist or a handy scapegoat. Aside from your partner in team competition, your caddie is your only source of advice. An asset for sure, but because he is part of your team, it is *you* who gets the penalty if your caddie should violate the Rules of Golf.

You certainly can accept advice from your caddie on what kind of shot to hit and even on how to hit it. He is even allowed to demonstrate the proper technique with a practice *swing*. But don't let him take a practice putt before you putt or test the surface of a bunker because it will "cost you."

Reading the greens and attending the flagstick are two common ways a local caddie can assist his player, but be sure he knows his responsibilities and limitations, because if he allows a putted ball to strike an attended flagstick, it's a penalty...and so is touching the green while pointing out the line of putt!

Your caddie should never touch your ball in play without your permission. If he does, it could prove costly. If your caddie, after finding a ball in the woods while searching for your errant drive, picks it up to see if it's yours, it will cost you a stroke if it turns out to be your ball. Same thing if your caddie "decides" that your ball is unplayable and picks it up before you have a chance to "declare" it unplayable.

Caddies carrying two bags are the rule, not the exception. So, keep in mind that if you are sharing a caddie with another player—be he a partner, foe or fellow competitor—the caddie will always be considered *your* caddie when *your ball* is involved in any Rules situation. And, all the equipment he is carrying is "deemed" to belong to you. So if *your* drive strikes either of the bags being *carried* by your caddie, *you* get the penalty. And, if the caddie accidentally moves a ball while searching in the rough, hope it's not yours because if it is you've just added one stroke to your score.

Laws for Loopers

A caddie is defined as "one who assists the player in accordance with the Rules, which may include carrying or *handling* the player's clubs during play." However, a caddie's typical duties often extend beyond simply carrying a bag, giving yardage and reading putts, especially if the caddie pulls a *double loop* or caddies for a group of four all riding in carts.

When a caddie is employed by more than one player, he is deemed to be the caddie of the player whose ball is involved. The equipment carried by him is deemed to be *that* player's equipment except when the caddie acts upon specific directions of the other player sharing the caddie, in which case he is considered to be *that* player's caddie. Whew! Now I wonder how I avoided costing my players a match during my looping days.

Here is a summary of the services a caddie *may* perform during a round.

- A caddie may search for the player's ball. Keep in mind that if the ball is moved by the caddie, the player suffers a penalty unless the ball was covered by sand (i.e., buried in a bunker).

- A caddie may repair old hole plugs and ball marks, but he must never touch the green to indicate the line of putt.

- A caddie may remove loose impediments on the line of putt or elsewhere. This means that it is okay for your caddie to brush away leaves or sand on the putting green with his hat, towel or hand, as long as he does not press down on the green. It also means that the caddie may assist the player in moving movable obstructions or large loose impediments that are not solidly embedded in the ground. Remember Tiger and the boulder?

- A caddie may mark the position of a ball but may not lift it, unless authorized by the player. In fact, a ball may only be lifted by the player, his partner or any other person *authorized* by the player.

- A caddie may always clean the player's ball when lifted from the putting green and any other time when the player is permitted to lift it, except: (1) When it was lifted because it assisted or interfered with another ball; (2) When it was lifted to determine if it was unfit for play; or (3) it was lifted for identification—although he may clean it to the extent necessary to identify the ball.

- A caddie may attend the flagstick while you putt. He can also help you line up to hit a "blind" shot by standing on the crest of a hill, or stand behind you to help with alignment, as long as he moves before you play your shot.

14 Clubs...(and No Borrowing One During the Round)

Did you know that there was a time when there was no limit to the number of clubs a golfer could carry? When Francis Ouimet won the 1913 U.S. Open, beating British greats Harry Vardon and Ted Ray in the process, he carried only seven clubs—or, rather, his 13-year-old caddie Eddie Lowery did. And, Winged Foot's Hall of Fame head professional Craig Wood often carried as many as 25! It was not until 1938 that the USGA established its 14-club limit, basing its policy on the fact that in those days the typical set of clubs used by the leading players included a No. 1 through No. 9 iron, a pitching wedge and sand wedge, two woods and a putter. Today, with wedge systems and "hybrid" clubs common, golfers must carefully select the right combination of clubs to suit their game and the course.

The penalty for starting a round with more than 14 clubs is severe (Rule 4-4). In stroke play, it's two strokes per hole for each hole you breach the Rule, with a maximum penalty per round of four strokes, which must be added to the scores for the first two holes. In match play, the penalty is applied to the state of the match at the conclusion of the hole at which the violation is discovered—and you get the penalty applied—even if you lose the hole. This means if you are carrying an extra club and lose the first hole you would be two down after having played only one hole!

The penalty is the same whether you carry one extra club or the Craig Wood collection. Whatever the number of excess clubs, once you discover that you are carrying too many, you must select the 14 you want, declare the others out of play immediately, and not use them again—or face disqualification.

Be careful if you discover *before* the round begins that you have too many clubs. You can't simply declare them out of play and carry them, anyway, as many golfers think. You must remove the excess from your bag and leave it—or them—behind (Decision 4-4c/1). However, if you begin a round with *fewer* than 14 clubs, you may add clubs to bring your total up to 14, but you may not borrow any club selected for play by another golfer playing the course, and you may not delay play acquiring or locating additional clubs.

There is no penalty if you find a club on the course and carry it back to the clubhouse in your golf bag, or if your caddie puts someone else's club, like a putter, into your bag *during the round*—just as long as you don't inadvertently play a stroke with that club (Decision 4-4a/15).

Damaged Goods

Play enough golf and chances are you've damaged a piece of your equipment during the course of a round. We're not talking about scuff marks on golf balls here, because your ball is not considered equipment under the Rules. Plus, most of us know you can always change balls between holes, and even *during* the hole if your ball becomes *unfit for play* while on that hole.

Equipment does include your golf glove, shoes, bag and clubs. The first three are simple: As long as you do not delay play, you are free to change gloves, shoes, and even your bag. Changing clubs, however, is a little different.

If one of your clubs is damaged in the *normal course of play*, during the *stipulated round*, (such as during your follow-through from under a tree), you may continue to use the club. You can also repair the club, or have it repaired, as long as it does not delay play. Additionally, if a club becomes unfit for play you can replace it with *any* club as long as you do not borrow a club selected for play by anyone else on the course. This means you can retrieve an extra club from your car trunk or your locker, but cannot use one of your playing partner's clubs as a substitute.

Let's take a moment to define a few of those terms. A stipulated round is 18 holes, unless a smaller number is authorized by the committee (in a nine-hole tournament or league, for example, the stipulated round would be nine holes). So, warming up *before* play is not during the stipulated round, nor is a *sudden death* playoff to decide a tie in stroke play. In match play, the stipulated round could be extended if the match were all square at the end of 18 holes.

With regard to club damage, the *normal course of play* is intended to cover all reasonable acts but specifically excludes cases of abuse. Making a stroke, practice swing or practice stroke; taking or replacing a club in the bag; using a club to search for or retrieve a ball; leaning on a club while waiting to play; teeing a ball or removing it from the hole; or accidentally dropping a club would all be considered in the normal course of play.

Now for the *ab*normal: Throwing a club in anger; slamming a club into a bag or intentionally striking something (a tree or the ground) with the club—other than during the stroke, practice swing or practice stroke—would *not* be considered within the normal course of play.

A club is unfit for play if it is substantially damaged (i.e., the shaft is dented, bent or broken into pieces; the club head becomes loose, detached or significantly deformed; or the grip becomes loose). A club is *not* unfit for play solely because the club's lie or loft has been altered, or the clubhead is scratched or dented.

Okay, now that the terms have been defined, you know that if during a stipulated round your club should become damaged, other than during the normal course of play, rendering it non-conforming or changing its playing characteristics, the club may not be replaced and may not be used for the rest of the round.

A player may use a club damaged prior to the round as long as the club, in its damaged state, *conforms with the Rules of Golf.*

So there you have it. If you start your round with the maximum of 14 clubs and one of them is damaged during the normal course of play, you can continue to play with the club, fix it or have it fixed, or replace if it's unfit for play. But if the damage was caused by a flare of anger and the club is unfit for play, you must immediately discontinue use of the club and you may not replace it. Temper, temper!

On "Conforming" Equipment

In 2000, the King, Arnold Palmer, shocked the world of organized golf by giving his endorsement for the use of a non-conforming driver to make the game "more fun" for beginners and "recreational" players.

There is nothing new about non-conforming equipment. It is easy enough to order over the Internet and you can see dozens of examples at the USGA Museum. In 2000, it only became a serious issue because, for the first time, it was being marketed by a legitimate golf equipment company and promoted by a national icon who not only shocked golfers throughout his "kingdom" but unintentionally challenged the authority of the United States Golf Association.

For more than a century the USGA has written and interpreted the Rules of the game. From their earliest days, in order to preserve the dignity and the challenge of the game, the Rules have included a description of the type of equipment that may be used. These Rules, along with the Rules of Play, while necessarily detailed and complex, have been voluntarily followed and championed by players from every playing level.

Some have argued that the game would be better served by two sets of Rules: one for the tournament player; and a less complicated (less comprehensive?) set for the casual player. I disagree. It may sound appealing on the surface but it cannot work.

For one thing, where would you draw the line between tournament play and casual play? Is your husband-wife event a tournament or casual play? How about your member-guest or the company outing? Does the most casual $2 Nassau remain casual when a dispute arises and the game is on the line? And how would I be able to compete, or compare my accomplishments, with those of my friends and rivals, or the King himself, if we were playing under different rules—by using different equipment.

Besides, while the game might be easier, would I really have more fun if I played with a non-conforming driver that had the potential to add a few yards to my occasional solid hit? Perhaps. Would the game be easier—and more fun—if I played with a square-grooved wedge? Maybe. What about a molded grip to correct that flaw or an adjustable 5-iron that could be reversed in the event I needed a left-handed club? Why stop there? The game might be "easier" if I purchased some hopped-up golf balls and tees that would make sliced or hooked tee shots a thing of the past—all of these items are non-conforming of course, but already available. And if you throw away the restrictions, I'm sure that over time they'll come up with a club to add another 40-50 yards to my tee shots and eventually come up with an "artificial" cure for my poor iron play.

This new game might be *easier*. But more *fun*? I don't think so. The great players are not great because of the equipment they play, and I don't want my good shots to be more the result of technology than flashes of skill. Who wins then— the guy who buys a better game or the guy with the talent and the desire to work on his game?

Come on. We all fell in love with the game for many of the same reasons: the challenge, the camaraderie, and the unlimited variety of sensational playing arenas. On this point keep in mind that, left unchecked, many of our great courses could be made obsolete and a proper challenge might require a course of 8,000 or 9,000 yards.

The USGA may not be perfect but no one can challenge their integrity or their commitment to the future of the game.

PART FOUR

Mixed Bag

Playing by Their Own Rules

I'VE HEARD MANY GOLFERS SAY THAT GOLF SHOULD HAVE two sets of rules—one for the professional tours, where men and women are earning their living, and another for the rest of us, as discussed earlier. I disagree. The Rules are complicated because of the wonderful complexity of the game and the incredible variety of playing arenas. However, while I don't think we need two sets of rules, I will admit that the pro tours, thanks to a number of special rules, do—and should—play a slightly different game.

Many of the differences have to do with the dramatic physical changes that must take place on a course hosting a Tour competition, and how those changes make that course different from when it is used for regular, everyday play. Because of these changes, the Tours use certain local rules that allow them to use the USGA Rules that the rest of us abide by, but also to create "specialized guidelines" that are necessary to cover circumstances brought about by unusual course conditions and a higher caliber of player.

For example, the very presence of large galleries creates changes to a golf course that make it different from the way it looks on a daily basis, and I'm not talking about the speed of the greens or the height of the rough. These changes primarily involve temporary immovable obstructions that have been erected to accommodate the crowds and structures such as tents, scoreboards, grandstands, and portable toilets. In addition, any temporary TV equipment built for members of the media is also classified as a temporary immovable obstruction, provided it is not mobile or otherwise readily movable.

Because of their temporary nature and the fact they are often placed very close to the primary playing area, special relief is allowed when temporary immovable obstructions interfere with play. This is in addition to the "standard" relief that you're entitled to if a permanent immovable obstruction interfered with your stance, the lie of your ball or the area of your intended swing. The difference is that with a *temporary*

immovable obstruction you are additionally entitled to relief
if the obstruction intervenes on a line between your ball and
the hole, or if the ball lies within one club-length of a spot
where this kind of intervention exists.

Other special tournament provisions include the so-called
one-ball rule, which is not really a rule of golf but rather
a local rule occasionally employed at the discretion of a
committee. Tour players who regularly play under the one-
ball rule are limited to the same brand and type of ball for the
entire round. You and I are not under any such limitation—
unless you are competing in an event and the committee has
announced that this local rule is in effect.

Another local rule the tours used at one time prohibited
players from touching their line of putt with a club. You and
I are permitted to remove sand, loose soil and other loose
impediments by picking them up or by brushing them aside
with our hand or club, or even sweeping them aside with a
towel or hat.

A local rule, used by the tours that many golfers mistakenly believe to be part of the Rules of Golf has to do with
embedded balls. An embedded ball is one that embeds or
"plugs" into its own pitch mark. Without a local rule, relief is

available for embedded balls only in the closely mown areas of the course. "Closely mown" means grass that is fairway height or lower—you do not get such relief in the rough.

Most golfers believe it is unfair to deny relief if their ball plugs in the rough and the USGA and PGA Tours agree. That's why the local embedded ball rule is *always* in effect for their events; however, it isn't "technically" in effect at *your* course unless your golf or tournament committee announces that it is. This is one local rule that I recommend for every club and every competition.

Winter Rules

In northern climes, the game of golf is usually thought of as a summer sport with Memorial Day and Labor Day heralding the beginning and the end of the season. There are, however, a growing number of golf addicts who look forward to a few additional holiday rounds of golf. What are you doing Christmas weekend and Presidents Day?

Few things short of an all-out blizzard will deter the winter golfer. Frozen tees, leaf-filled bunkers, even dreaded temporary greens are not enough to keep him away. Though the official Rules of Golf do not change as the temperature plummets, golfers often set their own version of the rules to deal with the harsh conditions they encounter.

The term "Winter Rules" or "Preferred Lies" are catch phrases used whenever the golfer is permitted to improve his lie in the fairway. Although discouraging their use during a district's "official season" (generally mid-April to mid-October) the USGA does suggest the language the committee should consider when abnormal conditions throughout the course interfere with fair play and necessitate Winter Rules.

These Winter Rules cover play adequately on the fairway but, as autumn leaves give way to snow flurries and the grounds crew puts the rakes away, closes the tees and opens the temporary greens, gaggles of winter birds create their own off-season rules. "Hurricane Rules," "Paradise Rules" and "The Leaf Rule" are just a few of the more interesting modifications.

Not surprisingly, the applications of these off-season rules vary greatly from course to course and often from group to group. Since few formal competitions are conducted during the winter and none of the scores affect the golfers' official Handicap Indices, there is little harm with the variety of rules until two golfers in the same group disagree on the interpretation of their own "rules." Since there is no publication or association with which to refer, settling disputes can be difficult.

It is not my intent to publish "Westmoreland's Winter Golf Rules" and the opinions expressed are simply that—opinions. But they are the opinions of a golf nut who once asked a couple, ice skating on a frigid January morning in front of the ninth tee at the Rye Golf Club, if it wasn't uncomfortably cold to ice skate, as I was searching for my golf ball in the frozen bullrushes. Following are some of my thoughts on winter golf....

Anywhere *through the green* the ball may be lifted, cleaned and placed within six inches of its original position, but not nearer to the hole. Since relief is being extended to balls in the fairway and rough alike, a strict distance limit should be set. Remember, the idea is to improve your lie on the rough turf, not change your shot.

When the ground is littered with leaves, I believe in using the "Leaf Rule" or at least what I call the "Modified Leaf Rule." When the ball is lost in an area where it would be reasonably expected to be found—were it not for the leaves—a ball may be dropped in a reasonable place without penalty. But, the player cannot *win* the hole—the best he can do is tie.

Winter Rule No. 3 deals with bunkers. When bunkers are no longer being maintained, I feel the player should be permitted to lift his ball, clear the area of debris, smooth the sand and return the ball to its *original* position.

If you are lucky enough to play your winter golf on regular putting greens, putt the ball out. If you're playing on temporary greens, I believe all putts should be conceded within a putter length of the hole, and I'm talking about a traditional-length putter.

Golfers should recognize that winter play is tough on the turf and take special care not to do any unnecessary damage. In particular, you should always tee off from the prescribed area, not from the Official Yardage markers. Concentrated play from the center of the teeing ground can do serious harm to the turf and make it impossible to put it in into first-class shape for the "other" season.

One last rule: If the ball picks up so much snow that it won't fit into the hole, the game is over.

On Handicaps

Your opponent is required to inform you of his correct Course Handicap, but from that point on the responsibility shifts to you. If the card is stroked incorrectly, giving you strokes on the wrong holes, or fewer strokes than you deserve, you will have to live out the consequences if you do not get the error corrected or make a timely claim.

In singles match play, the USGA recommends that the higher handicapped player get the full difference between the course handicaps of the two players. In four-ball match play, the recommendation is to reduce the course handicaps of all four players by the course handicap of the low handicapped player, who then plays at scratch. The other three players should play at 100% of the resulting difference. Here's an example. Ted and I are partners. Ted has a course handicap of 2 and I'm a 10. We're playing against Craig at 8 and Jim at 11. As the low handicapper, Ted plays at "scratch" reducing his handicap from 2 to 0. The rest of us reduce our course handicaps by 2, so I get 8 shots, Craig 6 and Jim 9.

In stroke play net competition, individual players should be allowed their full course handicap, which is deducted from their gross score at the end of the round. If Ted were playing in an individual net event his score card should show his gross score, minus his course handicap (74-2=72). In four-ball stroke play competition, men should play to 90% of their course handicap and women get 95%. In best ball of four, the allowances are 80% for men and 90% for women.

The USGA strongly endorses the idea that every golfer should play from the appropriate set of tees but this does not mean your group can't have a fair match even if one, or more, in the match play the forward or middle tees, and the others play the back tees. The procedure for equalizing the handicaps for players playing different sets of tees is the same as a match when a man plays against a woman.

Step one—each player converts his/her handicap index into a course handicap for the set of tees he/she wishes to play. Keep in mind that there is a *different* Course Handicap Table and *different* course rating for men and for women from *each* set of tees and that the differences in the Slope Ratings is worked into the Conversion Chart for each set of tees. For example: You, your mom and dad go for a family outing. Your mom and dad elect to play from the forward tees that have a course rating of 74.5 for women and 70.4 for men. You go to the *tips* which is rated at 73.4 for "He-men."

You refer to the Course Handicap Table for men from the "tips" and your index converts to a course handicap of 4. Your mom goes to the Forward Tee/*Women's* table and converts to a 10, and your dad uses the Forward Tee/*Men's* table and converts to a 5.

Step two—calculate the difference between the course ratings for the different set of tees and assign the player playing from the higher rated tees *additional* strokes equal to the rounded off difference.

Since your Dad is playing from the tees with the lowest course rating his course handicap remains at 5. The course rating from the tips is rated 3 strokes higher than the forward tee rating your dad must use (73.4—70.4 = 3) so you get to *add 3 strokes* to *your* course handicap for a total of 7. And, despite the fact that your mom and dad are playing from the same forward tees the *women's* course rating rounds off to 4 strokes higher than the *men's* course rating from those same tees (74.5—70.4 = 4.1) so mom gets 4 additional strokes for a total of 14.

Have fun and may the best man, or woman, win.

Outside Agencies

During The Players Championship, Brad Fabel hardly had time to exhale after successfully landing his tee shot on the 17th hole island-green before a bird, actually a herring gull, plucked his ball off the putting surface and dropped it into the surrounding lake. The ruling? The gull was an outside agency, so Fabel was required to place a ball at the exact spot from which the gull had lifted the other ball and play on without penalty.

Outside agencies include not only ball-lifting gulls, but all animate objects such as dogs, birds and other animals, walkers, joggers, the grounds crew, as well as moving golf carts and other vehicles. Have you ever been an outside agency? The answer is probably yes. If you have ever played, caddied or even sat in the bleachers at a tournament, under the Rules of Golf you've been an outside agency.

Can an outside agency affect play? The gull surely did. And if your ball has ever been deflected, stopped, played or simply taken by someone playing another hole, cutting grass or hunting for golf balls, then you too, have been affected by an outside agency.

Paul Simson *might* have been. Simson, an amateur from North Carolina, was 2-under par and one shot out of the U.S. Open first-round lead when his drive on the 10th hole found the tree-lined rough. After spending nearly five minutes looking in and around the trees, a spectator told Simson that another spectator had absconded with his ball. You must know or be virtually certain of the facts to be given relief under these circumstances, and the USGA official on the scene felt additional corroborating evidence was needed. "If maybe a couple of people had seen it happen, we would have given it some credibility," said the official. Denied relief, Simson had a lost ball, carded a triple-bogey 7, and ended up missing the cut by one shot.

If a ball in motion is deflected or stopped by an outside agency, there is no penalty—but you must play the ball wherever it comes to rest. Although this can mean playing from some pretty alien terrain, or even having to accept an out-of-bounds penalty, it can also mean good news if the agency in question deflected your ball onto the green or even knocks it into the hole. This actually happened on the PGA Tour when a big hitter drove his ball onto a par-4 green while the group ahead was still putting. His ball deflected off one of the guys on the green and went into the hole for an ace!

What if your ball were to somehow end up in or on the outside agency—say it bounced onto a mower that was cutting the fairway? You would be required to drop a ball as near as possible to the spot where the mower was when your ball came to rest upon it. Unfortunately, you do not get the advantage of any added "carry" provided by the vehicle.

When a ball in motion after a stroke on a putting green is stopped or deflected by an outside agency—say a dog darts out and grabs it—you must cancel the stroke, replace the ball and replay the stroke, all without penalty. If this should ever happen to you, enjoy it—it's one of golf's few authorized mulligans.

If your ball had come to rest and there was reasonable evidence that it was moved or taken by an outside agency, like the Fabel TPC airlift, there is no penalty. You would simply place the ball, or a substituted ball, on the spot from which it was plucked. If the ball was moved from a spot other than the putting green and you did not know the exact spot, then you would drop a ball as near as possible to the spot from where you estimate it was moved or taken.

Until now we have been dealing with *accidental* contact by an outside agency. The rules also provide for deliberate contact *through the green*. A judgment call must be made as to where the ball would have come to rest, always giving the player the benefit of the doubt. For example if a spectator intentionally stops a ball from bouncing over a green and the ball would have come to rest *either* in a water hazard or in the rough just short of the hazard, the player would be required to drop the ball in the rough just short of the hazard.

The Rules are necessarily complex because the game is played in and around nature herself. However, the Rules do provide fair relief even when an animate object interferes with play.

❧

The Golf Cart: Mobile Equipment

The golf cart changed forever the look of golf in America. Some applaud the cart for keeping the game accessible to those unable to walk for 18 holes. Others blame it for slowing the game down, and deplore the ribbons of blacktop on today's courses.

There's one thing they would agree on. If the Rules were hard to understand before the proliferation of carts, they were not made easier with their arrival.

The *Definitions in the Rules of Golf* tell us that "Equipment includes a golf cart, whether or not motorized. If a cart is shared by two or more players, the cart and *everything* in it are considered to be the equipment of the player whose ball is involved except that, when the cart is being *moved* by one of the players sharing it, the cart and everything in it are considered to be that player's equipment."

Yes, it's confusing, but perhaps best explained by looking at two common situations: A ball hitting a cart, and a ball being run over by one.

Let's say Mary and John are sharing a cart. They drive up to John's ball. John steps out, selects a club and promptly shanks one into the cart's front tire! Is John penalized?

Yes. His ball was involved, so the cart, and everything in it are considered his equipment. In stroke play, he plays his ball from where it comes to rest and adds a penalty stroke. In match play, he'd lose the hole. In a four-ball stroke play competition, the shanker still gets the one-stroke penalty, but his partner's score would *not* be affected. In four-ball match play the shanker would be disqualified *for that hole*. His partner may have reason to worry but is not penalized.

Now let's say that Mary is *driving* the cart when John hits it. According to the Definitions, the cart now is *her* equipment. However, if she is John's partner he still is penalized as noted above. If she is a fellow-competitor (stroke play) or opponent (match play) there would be no penalty imposed on either golfer because you are penalized only for hitting your own or your partner's equipment. In match play, John would have the option of playing the ball from where it came to rest or canceling the stroke and replaying it. In stroke play, he must play the ball from wherever it comes to rest. If the spot happens to be a water hazard or out of bounds, he would be subject to the appropriate penalty, just as he would benefit had his ball bounced into the hole.

If John's wayward shot strikes a cart used by anyone else on the course, the cart is not considered equipment but is an *outside agency*, and he must play his ball from wherever it come to rest without penalty. As noted above, if the ball ends up in the water hazard or out of bounds, the appropriate penalty would apply.

When a cart runs over a ball at rest, the ruling once again depends on who is in the driver's seat. If Mary and John are fellow-competitors in stroke play and John's ball is the victim, he incurs a penalty stroke if he is driving, but neither player is penalized if Mary is driving. If Mary is John's opponent in match play, then John is penalized one stroke if he is driving. She is penalized one stroke if she is driving—unless they are searching for John's ball, in which case there is no penalty.

If Mary and John are partners and a cart being used by their opponents runs over John's ball, the driver would be penalized one stroke unless they were helping to search for John's ball. There is no penalty if a cart driven by fellow competitors in stroke play runs over John's ball.

In all cases, when a ball at rest is moved it must be replaced. When a cart runs over a ball, it usually moves a very short distance—straight down—and significantly alters the lie! When this occurs *through the green* the ball must be placed in the nearest, most similar lie no closer to the hole, within one club length of the original lie, and not in a hazard.

If the lie wasn't altered when the ball was moved, you would simply replace the ball. If you can't tell from where the ball was moved, the ball should be dropped as near as possible to where you estimate the ball originally lay, no closer to the hole.

Drive carefully, or better yet, enjoy the walk.

Cleaning the Ball

A golf towel, slightly moistened, may have become as indispensable as a yardage book and an umbrella to today's well-prepared golfer.

I think all golfers know that when their ball comes to rest on the putting green they are always permitted to mark, lift and clean their ball. And, quite frankly, out of habit, most of us go through the process even when our ball is already squeaky clean.

Confusion can creep in and questions arise as to whether you can clean your ball under other situations. Rule 21, which deals exclusively with "Cleaning the Ball," is pretty specific. "A ball on the putting green may be cleaned when lifted. Elsewhere, a ball may be cleaned when lifted *except* if it has been lifted:

a. To determine if it is unfit for play.

b. For identification.

c. Because it is interfering or assisting with play."

So, when you lift your ball to take relief from *Ground Under Repair*, an immovable obstruction (like a cart path) or casual water, you *are* permitted to clean your ball. You can also do the wash and dry before putting your ball back into play after retrieving it from a water hazard, whenever you elect to declare it unplayable or if you happen to hit one OB.

Under the Rules, you are permitted to examine your ball at any time (as long as you notify your opponent and give him a chance to watch you lift and replace your ball) to determine whether it has become unfit for play (Rule 5-3). But while free to lift the ball to see if it is visibly cut, cracked or out of shape you are *not* permitted to clean it.

Similarly, under Rule 12-2, except when your ball comes to rest in a hazard, you may, if necessary, lift your ball to check it for identification purposes. In this case you may only clean it to the extent necessary to "ID" it as yours.

Finally, if your ball assists or interferes with the play of another ball you may be asked to lift it, and you must comply. However, when lifting your ball, you are not permitted to clean it before it is replaced, which may call for a two-finger "ice-tong" kind of grip on the ball to insure that you do not inadvertently clean it.

The reasoning behind denying, or limiting, your ability to clean a ball when lifted under these circumstances is very logical. You should not gain any advantage just because you're asked to move your ball, because you elect to check for identification marks or to see if it's damaged.

Must Have Gone in the Gopher Hole

A friend recently stopped me to ask if he had to consider his ball "lost" if he were unable to retrieve it from a gopher hole. I asked him if he could identify the ball as his while it was in the hole even though he could not extract it. He said he couldn't, so I asked him how he knew his ball had actually gone into the hole. "My caddie saw it go in!" "How close was your caddie to the gopher hole," I asked. "Oh, he was way out front, got a good view of it bouncing twice then watched as it disappeared!"

As inquisitive as I was—is as diligent you must be when a fellow competitor or opponent claims his ball "must have gone into a gopher hole," when he simply can't find it.

Rule 25-1-c deals with balls lost in common conditions like ground under repair; casual water and "certain" damage to the course—damage like the holes, casts or runways created by burrowing animals.

It may save you a stroke some day to know that just because you can't find your ball doesn't mean that it is a lost ball. In fact, if you "know" or are "virtually certain" that your ball is lost under one of these conditions covered by Rule 25, there is no penalty at all. However, before you can waltz off penalty free, you must provide the "knowledge" or explain the "virtual certainty" that the ball was, in fact, lost in ground under repair, casual water or a burrowing animal hole. You cannot simply *conclude* that it is because you cannot find it in the area you expected it to be. What is the threshold of "knowledge" and "virtual certainty" you ask? That's a good question.

My friend's caddie, or any other eyewitness, will usually provide all the evidence you'd need. Usually? Well, it might depend on the eyewitness' vantage point. If a ball were to disappear over the crest of a hill 220 yards from the tee and your caddie were standing on the tee next to you, his input might be meaningless. On the other hand if he had positioned himself 200 yards down the fairway and actually saw the ball disappear into a hole, you'd have ample knowledge.

USGA Decision 25-1c/1 deals with the "Knowledge and

Virtual Certainty" as it applies to Rule 25-1c. The question: A burrowing animal hole is surrounded by high rough and in a hollow not visible from the tee. A ball driven into this area is lost. The ball might be lost in the burrowing animal hole or it may be lost in the high rough. Is there knowledge or virtual certainty that the ball is lost in the animal hole? The USGA's answer was no. In such circumstances (because the ball *might* be in the high rough), there is not "virtual certainty, nor knowledge" that the ball is lost *in* the animal hole. Therefore the player must treat it as a "lost ball" and proceed under Rule 27-1 (Stroke & Distance).

Here's the bottom line. If the ball "might" be lost somewhere else—somewhere outside the ground under repair, casual water or burrowing animal hole—then you must treat it as a lost ball. But, if you have the kind of knowledge or can articulate the virtual certainty that will satisfy a competitive opponent, an inquisitive fellow competitor or a member on the "committee," you're entitled to relief without penalty.

Points Not Covered by the Rules: Do What's Fair
Let's not pretend that golf compares to skiing or hang-gliding

when it comes to the risk of bodily harm. But Aaron Baddeley's run-in with a six-foot alligator during The Players Championship in 2003 points out that even golfers can face some perilous situations.

Had Crocodile Dundee been carrying his bag, the Aussie could have simply let his mate remove the gator. However, both Aaron, and more so his caddie, were both happy to learn that relief was available with a rule and decisions covering life-threatening situations such as this and other not-so-deadly situations that one may encounter. Perhaps the all-time escape clause, Rule 1-4 is titled "Points not Covered by Rules" and reads: "If any point in dispute is not covered by the Rules, the decision shall be made in accordance with equity." In other words, if it isn't found in the Rules or in the *Decisions on the Rules*, it should be decided by what seems fair.

It may be a testimony to the thoroughness of the game's rulesmakers, the USGA and the R&A, that only a handful of decisions have ever been necessary under this "Rule of Equity." Perhaps the most common use has had to do with encounters like Baddeley's and other "dangerous" situations.

Many golfers have probably found their ball just after bumping into a low-hanging bee hive, or have discovered the pain a few fire ants can inflict. Some may have even had a face-off with a highly territorial swan or a bear that wandered onto the property.

Since the USGA has recognized that all of these situations, like the Florida alligator, could cause serious harm, Decision 1-4/10, allows the player to abandon the ball and to substitute another ball, without penalty, on the nearest spot which is neither nearer to the hole nor dangerous.

However, if the ball lies in a hazard, it must be dropped, if possible, in the *same* hazard and, if not, in a similar nearby hazard—but, in either case, not nearer to the hole. If it is not possible to do this, the player should drop a ball, under penalty of one stroke, outside the hazard, keeping the point where the original ball lay between the hole and the spot on which the ball is dropped.

It may be a matter of opinion, and even personality, when it comes to declaring a dangerous situation. The gator and the fire ants certainly qualify, but poison ivy or a cactus plant would not, even if the player fears the consequences of coming into contact with either. In some areas, it is not uncommon for golfers to come into contact with gigantic wasps, often called sand wasps, or cicada killers. Despite their fearsome appearance, the USGA has determined that they are known to be harmless, and free relief should not be allowed "in a situation where the Committee has published information" about these creatures.

Through the years, I've had a few encounters with dangerous situations—once a bear, mostly wasps and bees. I do recall a situation a few years ago during a Mixed Pinehurst Championship when a player saw what she swore was a large rattlesnake near her ball. The Metropolitan Golf Association's Executive Director, Jay Mottola and Jerry Mahoney, an acknowledged herpetophobe, were called on to render assistance. Jay and Jerry arrived on the scene, cautiously stepped out of their golf cart and slowly made their way into the margin of the woods, gauging every step. Our men got to within 30 feet of the ball, *saw the serpent*, made a quick about face and were heard saying, "you get relief" as their cart sped from the area.

The Velcro Rip (and Other Ambient Noises)

I had an acquaintance that I've credited with inventing what I call the Velcro Rip. This is a fellow for whom gamesmanship was an important part of his game. Eventually, of course, he ran out of people to play with. He went through the whole gamut of things that he could do that might distract an opponent or fellow competitor: shuffling around, jiggling coins in the pocket, standing too close. When people got used to all that, he'd time it perfectly where he could remove his glove with the r-r-r-rip just at the wrong time to distract someone while playing their stroke. This kind of behavior eventually wears thin, and people inevitably find someone else to play with.

The bottom line is that a golfer in his heart of hearts would not want to win if he knew that he'd done something outside the Rules. I think that is ingrained in the competitive spirit. Gamesmanship does sometimes come up, not much, but occasionally. In a junior context, I've talked to kids after the fact. There was one kid who appeared to be jiggling coins or keys in his pocket just when the other kid was trying to execute a shot. Or, he'd pick a spot to stand that could be distracting. I see it sometimes in casual play. You know the guy...he's the one who "reminds" you that you "missed the same putt yesterday" just before you are about to putt, or that "the OB really comes into play on this hole" just before an important drive.

When I talk to young people about the game, I always reinforce to them that the higher the level that you play on, the more respect you'll have for the Rules of Golf and the more important it will become to you (to observe them). I think this is borne out regularly, especially on the professional tours. The legends and the history of the game are filled with examples of players who have called penalties on themselves. If there's anybody out there who has a habit of getting a little edge (by, perhaps, working his Velcro Rip) they'll eventually have trouble getting a game.

Common Courtesy: A Part of the Game

No knocks on other sports, but one of the bragging points golf people like to boast about is the decorum of their game's players—from top flight touring pros to high handicap amateurs.

Through an era that has seen unprecedented growth in participant and spectator sports, trash-talking sports stars and steroid abuse, golf still demands that those who want to enjoy all the benefits the game has to offer must exhibit deportment, honor and integrity.

And while talent wins tournaments, golf remains one of the few games where etiquette is an integral part of the sport. First and foremost, we must all keep in mind that golf presents some potentially dangerous situations. After all, a drive can travel 300 yards or more and does not always go in the intended direction. So prior to playing a stroke or making a practice swing, you should always ensure that no one is standing close by or in a position to be hit by the club, the ball or any stones, pebbles or twigs which may be moved by your swing.

In the interest of all who play the game we should all play without delay. Arrive, get organized and be on the first tee at least 10 minutes before your tee time; be ready to play every time it is your turn to hit; walk at a brisk pace; putt out whenever possible; watch and take note of where every ball in your group comes to rest; play a provisional whenever necessary; and keep up with the group ahead of you, regardless of what may be happening behind you.

When you hit a ball into a sand bunker you should create as few footprints as possible by retracing your entry steps as you exit. And you should avoid entering or exiting a bunker other than at its nearest low point—never climb in or out over the high side of a bunker.

Once your ball is successfully extricated you should take care, and pride, that the bunker is properly raked and left in better shape than when you entered.

Through the green you should take care not to take divots on practice swings and to ensure that any divot you do create is properly replaced or filled. Once on the putting green, you should repair any ball marks you created and ensure that no one stands too close to the hole while attending or removing the flagstick, and when replacing it you should be sure you do not damage the lip of the hole and that the flagstick is centered in the hole.

Those who use golf carts should appreciate this privilege and recognize the potential damage they can create through careless use. Keep the carts away from wet areas, putting greens and teeing grounds and follow the regulations regarding the use of carts.

Golf is the greatest game—let's keep it that way.

Time Zone

Not long ago, I received a call from a golfer who accurately quoted Rule 14-2b: "In making a stroke a player must not allow his caddie, his partner or his partner's caddie to position himself on or close to an extension of the line of play or the line of putt." He reminded me that the Rules called for a two-stroke penalty in stroke play and loss of hole in match play, then asked a very direct question "Under what Rule is your opponent or fellow competitor penalized for the same violation?"

My answer both surprised and disappointed him because there is no Rule that would penalize a player for standing directly behind his opponent or fellow competitor while he plays a stroke! In fact, there would be no loss of hole or penalty strokes that could be assessed under the Rules of Golf were a player to jingle some coins or perform the "Velcro rip" at just the wrong time or do something else to interrupt or distract your ability to make a stroke, as obnoxious as those actions might be.

If there are no Rules that apply, what can you do in a situation where an opponent or competitor stands in a place that you find distracting? Step number one would be to let him know that you'd appreciate his not standing behind you, moving or making any noises when you are about to play. If that doesn't work you may have to resort to golf's secret rule—don't play with the guy again!

For tournament play, the USGA has strengthened the powers of the committee, who may disqualify a player for serious or repeated breaches of etiquette. The committee would also be justified if they rejected the culprit's entry the next time around.

Golf is one of the few sports that actually spells out a "code of conduct" for its participants. Etiquette may seem like something from another era, but it is taken very seriously by most golfers with the overriding principle that consideration of others should be shown on the course at all times.

As we welcome youngsters and new golfers from all walks of life into the game it is imperative that we all take the time to instruct them as to what is expected in the way of behavior. So just where should we stand when others are hitting? New Jersey PGA Hall of Fame pro Babe Lichardus liked to use the hands of a clock to help newcomers understand where to stand to avoid interfering with others. Understanding that the target line intersects the 12 and 6 on a clock-face, Babe would tell the kids to always stand "between 3:15 and 4:30" on the teeing ground. To this he would add, "and far enough away so that your shadow is out of the way too!"

Many golfers agree that the worst place for an opponent to stand is between 6:30 and 8:30 on the clock-face—just enough within the peripheral vision to be a nuisance. If you can't get to between about 3 and 5, then an alternative is to stand directly behind the player, at about 9 on the clock-face.

On the putting green, be sure to mark your ball if it might be a distraction to others and be very careful not to step on anyone's "line of putt." Once a player addresses his ball everyone should freeze and never, ever, stand between 10:00 and 3:00 or 5:00 and 8:00 on Babe's clock. This way you'll be in compliance with both the Rules and, just as importantly, the standards of etiquette.

❧

A Word about Golf Associations

In 1897, three short years after the United States Golf Association was founded, the first regional golf associations were organized and by the 1920's, independent, self-sustaining state and regional associations were in place across the nation.

Some of these amateur golf associations were founded for the purpose of establishing a handicap program, many were organized to conduct state or regional championships but all share the common mission to "preserve and protect the honorable traditions of the game of golf." Perhaps because these goals and aspirations are so similar to those of the USGA, it is often misunderstood and assumed that state and regional amateur associations are *part* of the USGA. Not so. These associations operate independently of the USGA, and each other, but they are tied together by their common commitment to golfers, clubs and the game and through an organization called the International Association of Golf Administrators (IAGA).

The voluntary relationship that state and regional amateur golf associations share with the USGA has flourished for over 100 years because of shared goals and "for the good of the game." The slogan is the USGA's but it clearly applies to amateur golf associations as well. In fact, former USGA Executive Director David Fay used to say that "the USGA could not carry out its mission without the assistance, cooperation and talents of the state and regional amateur golf associations."

Take for example the 13 USGA national championships. For the U.S. Open alone, the USGA requires the use of more than 100 courses across the country and the talents of 10 times that number of men and women volunteers to prepare, organize and conduct golf's most important championship. This work is done primarily by state and regional amateur associations. Similarly, guidelines for course measurement and course rating, education on etiquette and the Rules of Golf, regulation on the rules for amateur status and standards for pace of play are all established by the USGA, but processed, installed and promoted by state and regional amateur golf associations.

These state and amateur golf associations are meeting their mission with high marks. Golfers certainly recognize the meaningful and historic championships they conduct, along with their communication efforts via quality publications and Web sites. In addition, they provide a host of behind-the-scenes, day-by-day assistance to clubs and golfers of all ages and ability levels.

Often overlooked is the vital work these associations do to ensure the future of the game. At the forefront are programs for junior golfers, turf research and a host of educational programs. Through charitable foundations, many associations have also created innovative programs like career-oriented intern programs and inner-city alternative golf facilities and distributed millions of dollars worth of college scholarships to deserving caddies and youngsters who have an interest in golf. These meaningful and worthwhile programs have helped to open up the game to a broader segment of our population and will help ensure the game's future, but they have not received much national publicity because of golf associations' independent and localized status.

The USGA Handicap System enables golfers of every level to compete fairly with each other and is one of the reasons for the game's enduring popularity. It is in this area that state and regional amateur golf associations have made their greatest contribution to golf. In many areas of the country this service has been going on for more than 60 years and in most cases represents golf associations' most important and widely used service. State and regional associations have made it their responsibility to ensure that the handicap system for the entire nation functions in accordance with USGA guidelines and that it is properly monitored and controlled.

It should be recognized, and appreciated, that fees charged by non-profit state or regional amateur associations are not just handicap fees. Rather, they are membership dues—dues that are plowed right back into the game of golf in the form of meaningful services.

State and regional associations were there at the beginning and, with the USGA, will continue their unheralded yet vital role to provide the best possible services for golfers simply "for the good of the game." They deserve your support.

Afterword

For when the One Great Scorer comes
To mark against your name,
He writes—not that you won or lost—
But HOW you played the Game.

—GRANTLAND RICE, 1908

WHILE GEORGE STEINBRENNER, LEO DUROCHER AND Tanya Harding might disagree, and Tiger may figure his career came up short with anything less than 19 "majors," in the real big picture I think Mr. Rice had it right—when it comes to golfers. For most of us the club championship, much less a Masters title, are far out of reach but we are just as passionate about the game.

How would you define what being a "good golfer" is all about? Is it simply someone who consistently shoots a low score, or is it someone who plays the game the right way? I love to play with low handicap players but for me it goes way beyond a guy's handicap or score, it's someone who practices good etiquette, someone who cares about the course and his companions, is courteous and fun to be around. Someone for whom pace of play is not a challenge, someone who's a pleasure to be with. That's my definition of a good golfer.

My wife likes repeating this story. My old friend and *consigliere* Arnie is now an active and avid golfer but before he took up the game he insisted that I first tutor him as to the game's etiquette. He looked forward to the day when he could play some business golf and did not want to embarrass himself when playing with more experienced and accomplished golfers. I assured him that as long as he stood in the right place, trained himself to watch where his—and others'—balls went, was ready to play when it was his turn, that *anyone* could enjoy a game with him.

In my experience, the only time I don't enjoy a new playing partner is when he or she is constantly whining about their poor play, needs help finding their ball after *every* shot and is never ready to play when it's their turn. In other words, when they interfere with others' enjoyment of the game. I haven't played with my friend Sears in quite a while but we used to play regularly. At one point his handicap had soared over 20 and he apologized by saying, "it must be tough playing with me!"

"No it isn't! I love playing with you." He was a laugh a minute, kept pace, and never groused over his play. We had a ball every round, they were invariably fun, occasionally memorable and that's part of why we play, isn't it?

Believe me, with the possible exception of your partner, nobody really cares what you're shooting and, unless they are the group's scorekeeper, nobody really knows what you're shooting—unless *you* constantly bring it up! They can, and will, enjoy your company as long as you participate in the banter, play by the rules and observe, and embrace, the traditional courtesies that have served the game so well for so long.

Enjoy the game.

 *Advance Praise for*
A Game for Life

Gene Westmoreland—with his pleasantly crisp writing style—does a swell job in educating and entertaining the reader on the basics and nuances of the Rules of Golf. Kudos.

—David Fay, former Executive Director
of the United States Golf Association

A different and wonderful look into the rules of golf. It's a mixture of the decisions book and the rule book. With specific tournament examples and humor, this is a must read for anyone looking to better understand the rules of the game.

—Johnson Wagner, PGA Tour Professional

Finally a golf rules book that gets it "right." And that means a thorough discussion of the most useful rules without needing an official standing by to translate. I've had the privilege of playing plenty of golf with Gene and he has the same rare and simple manner in deciphering the rules in person that he does in the book. And it all comes to light amid his passionate storytelling. My decision: "enough practice swings at the rules... read it and REALLY impress your golf pals!"

—Dan Hicks, golf announcer, NBC Sports

Playing by the rules, self-imposing penalties and exhibiting proper etiquette is at the core of why golf is considered a gentleman's game. Unfortunately, most golfers do not know many of even the most basic rules by which golf is played, which is a shame yet understandable given the great breadth and complexity of the rules of golf. Gene Westmoreland has always been my go-to-guy for any rules related questions that I have had, so I am not surprised that he has written a golfer-friendly book that can help anybody to better understand the rules of this incredible game that so many of us love. After reading Gene's book, I immediately gave it to my 16-year-old son and told him to read it!

—Ken Bakst, 1997 USGA Mid-Amateur
Champion and owner-founder of Friar's Head

Gene is a tremendous ambassador of golf. Golf in the Metropolitan New York area has benefitted from his passion for competition, and his respect for the rules and traditions of the game. Now, Gene has found a way to transfer his love of the game to the pages of this book. In *A Game for Life*, Gene presents the rules in a charming fashion, and weaves in some great quotes and stories. A great read for golfers and for those looking to learn and enjoy this great sport.

> —*Brian A. Crowell, PGA Head Golf Professional at Glen Arbor Golf Club6 and host of The Clubhouse radio program, WFAS (New York)) and broadcaster and analyst for NBC and CBS golf coverage.*

A Game for Life simplifies learning and understanding golf's rules. It will be enjoyable reading for everyone who loves the game.

> —*Doug Steffen, Head Professional, Baltusrol Golf Club*

Gene has given us a light, fun way to understand the rules of golf. His anecdotes and stories mixed in with the rules make an easy read for golfers of all skill levels. His experiences as a rules expert and tournament director for the MGA make

Gene a perfect guy to help us all enjoy the game! Gene likes
his playing partners to play fast, enjoy the game and play by
the rules! I'm glad we have guys like Gene to help us learn
how to do it.

—*Jack Druga, Head Golf Professional, Shinnecock Hills*

For those of us who have thumbed aimlessly through the
Rules of Golf, help has arrived. Gene Westmoreland, an expert
on the Rules of Golf, has given us a simple, logical, memorable—and enjoyable—approach. Neither dry nor lecturing,
it is eminently entertaining and enjoyable. Mr. Westmoreland
does not set out to challenge or replace the of confounding
and bewildering Rules of Golf; rather, he teaches us how to
navigate it, and encourages us to make it our "15th club."
He gives plenty of common and not-so-common examples
of situations in which golfers find themselves, and leads us
effortlessly through the Rules of Golf in each instance so that
we may handily find the answer as to how to proceed. He
even covers such things as the "Velcro Rip," an act of gamesmanship some of us have encountered from a particularly
competitive (and usually inept) player. Many thanks to Mr.

Westmoreland for bringing us *A Game for Life*. Every golfer, from scratch to 36, will enjoy and profit from reading it.

—*Deborah Jamgochian, 15-time women's*
club champion, Winged Foot Golf Club

A Game for Life proves that golf is a metaphor for life. In it, Gene Westmoreland manages to condense the Rules of Golf so the average golfer can relate. The rules come alive through his everyday examples and sense of humor; indeed, he knows that everyone who plays this game needs a few laughs. Westmoreland also illustrates that composure, humility, sense of humor, and concern for others are important in golf as they are in life, and his definition of a "good golfer" will put a smile on many faces, especially those who do not par that often. Golfers of all skill levels will feel more confident about the Rules of Golf after this informative and easy-to read book. In addition, this book just reminds us of why we all love the game.

—*Beth Post, President of the Women's*
Metropolitan Golf Association and former
President of Quaker Ridge Golf Club

 *About The MGA Foundation*

The mission of the MGA Foundation is to help build a foundation for the future of golf here in the Met Area. We pursue the mission through a number of activities, including our GOLFWORKS student intern program, annual Caddie Academies, Rules and Etiquette workshops for high school golfers and their coaches and support of other area junior programs. The Foundation was also a co-founder, along with the Met PGA, of the First Tee of Metropolitan New York which has grown into the largest First Tee Chapter in the country with facilities throughout the Tri-State area. Each year thousands of young people benefit from these programs and are introduced to the character building and life lessons that golf teaches us all.

In addition, the Foundation holds educational seminars on the Rules of Golf, Pace of Play, Golf Course Maintenance and Environmental Issues. It conducts annual Presidents Council and Public Golf Forums, as well as a biennial Club Operations Survey for leaders of the local golf community. The Foundation has also created a library and display area to preserve the rich history of golf in the Met Area at its headquarters "Golf Central" in Elmsford, NY.

Part of the proceeds for the sale of every copy of *A Game for Life—Golf's Rules and Rewards* will benefit the Foundation. The MGA Foundation is a 501 (c)(3) charitable organization funded solely by donations from the local golf community. For information, or to make a donation, call 914-347-GOLF, or go to www.mgagolf.org.

MGA Foundation . . . Golf Grows Here